B.C.I.T. LIBRARY

000204189
PN 1998 A3K737
c.1

70871

SO-CDP-738

A3K737

THE FILMS
OF
STANLEY KUBRICK

by Daniel De Vries

William B. Eerdmans Publishing Company
Grand Rapids, Michigan

LIBRARY
B. C. INSTITUTE OF TECHNOLOGY
BURNABY 2, B. C.

Copyright © 1973 by Wm. B. Eerdmans Publ. Co.

All rights reserved

Library of Congress Catalog Card No.: 72-84009
ISBN: 0-8028-1481-6

Printed in the United States of America

For Sharon, without whom going
to the movies wouldn't be half the fun.

Contents

Acknowledgments

Special thanks to

United Artists, UA:16, for the use of prints of *The Killing* and *Paths of Glory*;

Columbia Cinematheque, for information making it possible to view *Dr. Strangelove* reasonably close to home;

Ferris State College in Big Rapids, Mich., for a special screening of *Dr. Strangelove*;

Films, Inc., of Skokie, Ill. for a special screening of *Lolita* in their offices;

and the staff of The Museum of Modern Art, in New York, who gave me tickets to their Kubrick Retrospective during the 1971-72 holiday season and were a good deal kinder and more helpful than a small-town boy expects New Yorkers to be.

70871

Introduction

The impressive thing about Stanley Kubrick's films is that they are, on the one hand, visual art as movies must be, and on the other, works that deal with ideas. One might often disagree with Kubrick's ideas, at times even find them a bit silly, but none of that detracts from the fact that Kubrick puts together picture shows which are entertaining, aesthetically pleasing, and provoking, all at the same time.

Kubrick is, among other things, a true screen poet. He knows how to use visual images to communicate. Movies should probably never communicate anything with words that could be communicated with a picture, and Kubrick's rarely do. Kubrick characterizes a gangster by the way he handles a gun in *The Killing*, a strange family triangle with a peck on the cheek in *Lolita*, a mad general by the way he chomps his cigar in *Dr. Strangelove*. What is wonderful about Kubrick's imagistic skill is that theme and image conjoin so naturally in his movies. In *Paths of Glory* soldiers attacking a hill called "The Anthill" really look like ants and Kubrick has the good sense not to have anyone verbalize the comparison. In *Dr. Strangelove* the top half of the screen above a group of government officials is completely black and one does not have to say or think "impending doom"—one feels it. The genius in all of this is that none of it is artificially imposed upon the movie. To say, for example, that the high ceilings in *Citizen Kane* symbolize, in the sense of merely signifying or standing for, Kane's vaunting ambition is a completely inadequate explanation of the artist's work. What Orson Welles has done in that movie is to make his viewers *feel* Kane's upward striving without even thinking in terms of symbols. This is one facet of Kubrick's genius—his ability to project theme without using symbols, by creating visual images which *are* the themes of his films. In doing this Kubrick has created a screen world of his own. This can be both an artistic liability and an asset. On the one hand it leaves him free to move at will, but on the other hand there must be touch-points between his world and ours, or we will not understand or appreciate his.

The Kubrick world is not exactly a pleasant place. It is marked by belief in the badness of human nature, and the suggestion that there is at work in the universe some malevolent force, whose chief aim is to destroy human beings and their expectations. Even in *2001: A Space Odyssey*, certainly his most optimistic film, salvation does not come to man as man, but through man's evolution into something else. In *Lolita* Quilty personifies that force, in *Dr. Strangelove* it is the film's namesake, but in other films it goes unspecified and unnamed. But one knows that it is there because things never work out. It is something like the Lord of the Flies. As the head asks Simon in Golding's novel, "I'm the reason why it's no go? Why things are what they are?" Maybe in Kubrick's work as in Golding's, the problem is that the beast is in all of us. Kubrick is a chess lover, and critics often point to chess motifs in his movies. In general the comparison holds up—Kubrick's movies are like chess games with an unseen opponent who always wins.

In recent films, notably *Dr. Strangelove* and *2001* (also *A Clockwork Orange* if one wishes to consider the Ludovico treatment mechanistic), Kubrick uses machines extensively, even as characters. His idea does not seem to be so much the glorification of technology—certainly he does not suggest that technology will save man from anything—but rather a personal fascination with the logicality and dependability of machines, compared to humanity's propensity to blunder. Kubrick's machines don't always do what men want them to do, but they do do what they are supposed to do, according to their own built-in implacable logic. If they hurt men they can self-righteously plead innocence, as HAL does in *2001*, by blaming "human error." Their "mistakes" are always "traceable to human error."

Because Kubrick's films are set in his own world, and because he sees man as a loser, one sometimes misses humanness in his characters. Some filmmakers, especially many of the French and Czech New Wave directors (Francois Truffaut and Milos Forman come to mind as the best examples of each) make great movies by thoroughly involving the viewer in the everyday lives of very human characters. This is something Kubrick does not do. Thus his movies are more stylized than realistic art. If one is partial (as I am) to humanist art, he tends to think of Kubrick's anti-humanism as a limitation, although, seen more objectively, it is probably merely a matter of taste.

Aside from the skill with images they consistently exhibit and certain recurring motifs, Kubrick's films are remarkably different from each other. They range from the starkly black and white (*Paths of Glory* and *Dr. Strangelove*) to the riotously colored (*2001*); from the lightning-paced (*Dr. Strangelove*) to the ponderous (*Lolita*); from the frivolous but fun (*The Killing*) to the idea-ridden (*2001*); from the bravura-performanced (*A Clockwork Orange*) to the realistically acted (*Paths of Glory*) and to the nearly actorless (*2001*); from the realistically set (*Paths of Glory*) to the futuristic (*A Clockwork Orange*). Needless to say, each is best dealt with specifically, and that is what the following essays attempt to do.

1

The Killing

Stanley Kubrick made his first film at the age of twenty-one.[1] A short documentary about a boxer, entitled *Day of the Fight*, it was sixteen minutes long and cost $3,900—one tenth the length and about one four-hundredth the cost of *2001: A Space Odyssey*. RKO bought it for a little more than it cost to make, and Kubrick, then working as a photo-journalist for *LOOK* magazine, quit his job to become a movie director.

Before the advent of the film school, that was how a film director got his start, and for Stanley Kubrick, who had done badly in high school and never attended college, learning how to make a movie was an on-the-job sort of thing. He learned technical photographic skills while working for *LOOK*, but considers himself fortunate to have gotten out when he did. "The stuff I had been shooting at *LOOK* was pretty meaningless," he says. "What kind of photography can you do on a college costume party or on stories like 'Is an Athlete Stronger Than a Baby?'"[2] British critic Alexander Walker suggests another source of education: "In Kubrick's case there appears to be a very strong creative link between chess and the camera—one is a mental discipline, the other an imaginative craft."[3] Certainly Kubrick learned to use his mind in disciplined fashion somewhere. His films are usually carefully planned and impeccably shot.

[1] I am indebted for biographical data to Alexander Walker's book *Stanley Kubrick Directs*.

[2] Kubrick, quoted by Zimmerman, "Kubrick's Brilliant Vision," p. 31.

[3] Walker, *Stanley Kubrick Directs*, p. 11.

He followed *Day of the Fight* in the same year (1951) with *Flying Padre*, a nine-minute film about a Roman Catholic missionary pilot with a huge Southwestern parish. In 1953, for $30,000, he and Howard Sackler (*The Great White Hope*), who wrote the script, made a feature film called *Fear and Desire* about four lost soldiers in an unspecified war. Kubrick himself now calls it "undramatic and embarrassingly pretentious,"[4] but the experience was invaluable.

> Today, I think that if someone stood around watching even a smallish film unit, he would get the impression of vast technical and logistical magnitude. He would probably be intimidated by this and assume that something close to this was necessary in order to achieve more or less professional results. This experience and the one that followed with *Killer's Kiss*, which was on a slightly more cushy basis, freed me from any concern about the technical or logistical aspects of filmmaking.[5]

That next film, *Killer's Kiss*, made in 1955, has held up better, and unlike *Fear and Desire* is still being distributed. It is basically an action film about "a girl who is kidnapped by the sadistic owner of a dance hall and rescued from his clutches by a gallant young boxer."[6] Kubrick compares the two this way:

> While *Fear and Desire* had been a serious effort, ineptly done, *Killer's Kiss*... proved, I think, to be a frivolous effort done with conceivably more expertise, though still down in the student level of filmmaking.[7]

From here, Kubrick moved into partnership with James B. Harris, a talented and financially well-connected young producer, and worked with him on his next several films. Their first effort was *The Killing*.

The Killing is an engaging gangster picture which starts out rather slowly with scene-setting, but unwinds into a positively entertaining melodrama of big plans and frustrated expectations. In later films Kubrick takes on subjects like the destruction of the world, and the evolution of man from ape to god—here he is merely concerned with presenting a well-made entertainment, and on those terms the film is certainly a success.

---

[4] Kubrick, quoted by Walker, p. 17.   [6] Walker, p. 18.
[5] Kubrick, quoted by Walker, p. 18.   [7] Kubrick, quoted by Walker, p. 18.

The cast of *The Killing* consists mainly of stock supporting actors who have since faded from the memories of everyone but film fanatics. Two exceptions are Sterling Hayden, who reappears in *Dr. Strangelove*, and Vince Edwards of *Ben Casey* fame, who receives a top billing but appears only briefly.

Hayden plays an archetypal punk named Johnny Clay who masterminds a very imperfect but highly promising racetrack robbery, one of several "killings" in the film. He comes on with an exaggerated, tight-lipped bravura—when he does nothing else he looms menacingly.

Hayden's gang is a mixed bag of larcenous, but previously noncriminal and respectably lower-middle-class, drudges who all need money. The contrast between their collective banality and their grandiose plans is one of several amusing ironies in *The Killing*, and although this film is certainly no message-movie, it introduces us to the comic, ironic, and frequently cynical view of mankind that marks all of Kubrick's work. Excepting Col. Dax in *Paths of Glory*, and Spartacus, there are no classic heroes in Kubrick's work, and significantly, both of those men are eventually defeated by a world unfriendly to heroic types.

Actually, except for Johnny Clay, the characterization of the thieves in *The Killing* borders on the maudlin. One (Joe Sawyer) is a bartender at the racetrack whose wife is dying from an incurable disease. Another (Ted de Corsia) is a cop in trouble with the mob. A third (Jay C. Flippen) is an aging homosexual who has a thing for Hayden. The fourth (Elisha Cook), the weakest link in Hayden's schemes, is a racetrack cashier, an ineffectual little man, panicky at the thought of losing his bitchy, ugly, and glamor-deluded wife (Marie Windsor).

The scenes between these last two, George and Sherry Peatty, are also the weakest parts in the film. Their relationship is pathetically funny—Sherry's pretentions and George's fawning over her might have provided some comedy—but they are treated more-or-less seriously, and neither is the sort of character an audience receives sympathetically. Her veiled threats and recriminations, and his desperation, quickly become silly and boring. Kubrick wrote the screenplay, and Jim Thompson contributed "additional dialogue"; in George and Sherry's scenes it crackles with lines like "Why did you ever marry me anyway?" and "I know I can trust you, Sherry."

But the film begins to move after Kubrick has introduced the conspirators and their problems, and Hayden goes in search of two thugs who must perform independent paid assignments without knowing the gang's plans. One, a magnificent muscle-bound, Russian-émigré, professional wrestler, chessplayer, and rumble starter, is played wonderfully by Kola Kwariani, who makes humorous good use of total verbal incoherence. His part in the scheme is to start an attention-diverting brawl at the track bar, an assignment he fulfills with a vengeance, flipping six track cops hither and yon with gleeful abandon.

The other paid hood is played by Timothy Carey, who also appears with an outstanding performance in *Paths of Glory*. He must shoot down a favored thoroughbred in the seventh race on the day of the heist. The first scene between Carey and Hayden is a delight. With a corny but somehow effective touch, Kubrick casts Carey as a gun- and animal-loving fellow who is cooling his heels on a farm. He gently strokes a puppy, while Hayden blasts away at dummy policemen with a horrific repeating shotgun which Carey has modified for him. Carey's part will be a snap, Hayden assures him—the worst anyone can touch him for is shooting horses out of season.

There is also a later notable scene involving Carey. He arrives at a track parking lot early in order to get a front-row position at the final turn, but the Black attendant will not let him drive in until another parking lot—presumably one without a good sniping position—has filled. Carey pleads that he is a paraplegic and likes to watch races from his car. He bribes the attendant, who interprets his persuasive zeal as liberal friendliness, and later decides to watch the seventh race with him. At this, Carey turns on him, telling him to know his place, and the attendant stalks off growling, "*My* mistake." Considering that *The Killing* was made in 1956, when Black appearances in Hollywood films were primarily for sniggering comedy, the racial honesty of the scene is remarkable, and in comparison

12

with the pained liberalism of more recent Hollywood treatments of race, the scene strikes home on racism as the soap-operish platitudes of films like *Raisin in the Sun* and *Guess Who's Coming to Dinner?* have consistently failed to do. When the actual robbery sequences begin, Kubrick and his editor, Betty Steinberg, have a field day. The scheme for the killing is complicated, and six different people must fulfill various duties precisely on schedule. Thus, the cutting back and forth and the jumping forward and backward in time become rather complex, and Kubrick comes through with a sophistication which belies his years and relative inexperience.

Several times the start of the seventh race is announced and finally the conspirators scurry through their rounds, culminating with Kola Kwariani's magnificent brawl; Carey's equicide; and Hayden, disguised in the rubber mask of a drunk and wielding his super-shotgun, overseeing a frantic clerk who stuffs thousands of loose bills into an outsized canvas bag.

Suspense builds through all of this as Kubrick plays manipulator in the best Hitchcockian tradition—throwing out red herring after red herring as Hayden's hare-brained scheme, incredibly, succeeds. By this time, for all of Hayden's bravado, the audience knows that the plot has no right to succeed, and the effect is not only suspenseful but comic as the crooks bumble along. Mike, the track bartender who has carried Hayden's gun to the track in a flower box, overzealously guards his posies and clunks them around the employees' locker room as though he were wearing a ball and chain. Wally Unger, the homosexual, who was supposed to stay miles away from the track, turns up thoroughly plastered to see how things are going. The cop runs away from a woman pleading for his help, in order to get to the track in time for his move. George and Sherry have quarreled, and George, who suspects Hayden of cuckolding him, is all righteous anger and agitation.

Kubrick finishes the gang and the film off with perverse twists that foreshadow *Dr. Strangelove*. Vince Edwards, who has *really* been cuckolding George and knows the whole scheme from Sherry, appears at the divvy-up session before Hayden, and proceeds to blast the gang to kingdom come. Then George staggers out of the kitchen, where he has been drinking, and kills Edwards. Badly wounded, he nevertheless somehow gets home to Sherry, who expects Edwards and a few hundred thousand dollars. George shoots her, before going down himself beneath a tipped-over parrot cage. Sherry, unrelenting in her passion for bad lines, dies groaning, "It's a bad joke without a punchline." The carnage, if not quite so graphic and prolonged as the famous sixties massacres in Arthur Penn's *Bonnie and Clyde* and Sam Peckinpah's *The Wild Bunch*, is perversely effective. Unlike *Bonnie and Clyde*, here one hardly sympathizes with the victims. In fact he rather feels that they have it coming. It is poetic justice in a black humor vein. In *A Clockwork Orange*, Kubrick's prepossession with black humor becomes so grand and glorious that it is offensive and boring; perhaps there is something about black humor which necessitates a small-scale, low-key approach. In this film the slaughter as climax is strangely satisfying. Considering all that these crooks went through to get where they are, it is all painfully funny, the punchline of a really good, if slightly scary, joke. In the later film the steady diet of stomp and snuff gets nauseating.

A special comeuppance is reserved for Hayden, and in his case it is a fate worse than death. He has the money, and when he comes to the apartment and realizes there's a massacre going on upstairs, he takes off carrying a huge ancient suitcase bursting with banknotes. He and his waifish girlfriend (Coleen Gray) arrive at the airport suitcase in hand, and after a hassle with an airline official who refuses to let them take the thing into the passenger compartment of the plane, they watch wistfully as the loot rides to the plane, perched precariously on a baggage truck. Predictably, it falls to the runway and breaks open, and our hero watches as several hundred thousand dollars, blown by propeller wind, scatter to the four corners of the airport. It's a nice touch: we like Hayden too much to see him killed in an ordinary gunfight, but, no question, he has this coming.

The Killing is photographed by Lucien Ballard, one of Hollywood's better cinematographers. His racetrack sequences are particularly good, communicating the tension of the event. The mundaneness of the conspirators comes through effectively in his treatment of their homes and neighborhoods— plain, ugly, and filled with bric-a-brac. In one scene we see the conspirators conspiring, drinking, and (except for George Peatty) smiling through a smoky haze, as though they were about the Wednesday-night poker game, not grand larceny.

One ought not make too much of a film like *The Killing*. It is filmed on a small scale, and unlike most of Kubrick's other work, it is intended mainly as an entertainment. Nonetheless, the director shows us things which we will see more of as we watch his films. One of these is his basically negative, but comic, view of mankind. Everybody in *The Killing* gets killed or busted, but it is a funny movie, and not a sad funny movie in the Truffaut tradition either. *The Killing* invites contrast with *Shoot the Piano Player*. In that gangster film Truffaut also gives us people who are unsuccessful. But because he cares about them so passionately, we care too; and although it is a very funny movie, their eventual failure is positively heartrending. Our hearts are not much rent in *The Killing*, largely because Kubrick, unlike Truffaut, keeps his emotional distance from his characters, as he must if his comic effect is going to work. It is a film about losers. Their success is contrary to every law of the universe, and we laugh, not only because of that, but because each success simply postpones the inevitable failure. When the end comes, we are left with a pile of bodies that eliminates denouement, and after that first gasp at the carnage, it seems as humorous as the smashed autos at the end of a Keystone Kops film.

It is, of course, humor of a very black sort, and later Kubrick will adapt or collaborate with such noted black-humor writers as Vladimir Nabokov and Terry Southern. But that is well in the future in 1956, and although black humor is certainly around, the movie-going public has not been exposed to the large doses which it will get, both in movies and in real life, in the sixties. Coming when it does, *The Killing* is remarkable for its nastiness. One senses in watching this film that Kubrick is working mostly by instinct—that the black touches, which

15

become intellectualized into a sort of dogma in *Dr. Strangelove* and *A Clockwork Orange*, are still at a gut-level stage in *The Killing*. Thus, although it sounds like a contradiction in terms, there is an innocence about the perversity in *The Killing*. It is a much less polished and entertaining film than *Dr. Strangelove*, but one feels that although he does not care much for the people he is watching, they are, after all, real people. We certainly do not respond to the later bomb comedy this way. The lack of intellection in *The Killing* provides it with much of its life, and given Kubrick's later tendency to overintellectualize, one wishes that a bit of this innocence had been retained.

At any rate, Kubrick's voice in *The Killing* is the voice which we have come to identify with his later films. There is none of the liberal idealism of *Paths of Glory* or *Spartacus* here, but rather the cynical humor of *Dr. Strangelove* and *A Clockwork Orange*.

2

PATHS OF GLORY and SPARTACUS

Paths of Glory is a powerful film. It is controlled and taut, and builds to a peak of great dramatic excitement. It is one of those rare films which simply do not lag, and which everything feels right about. This, all the more remarkable since for a war movie it has little war action. Instead it is a study of several personalities and a society.

It is commonly referred to as a pacifistic film, but much more important than its indictment of war is its indictment of class brutality and officer irresponsibility in the French army during World War I. That Kubrick made it at age thirty is noteworthy because of the maturity which he displays in handling technical aspects of production, seasoned actors like Kirk Douglas and Adolphe Menjou (whose presence in the film is especially ironic since he was one of Hollywood's most noteworthy right-wingers), and weighty themes—all at a time when there simply were no directors that age making major films.

Making a protest film is a difficult art. There is a great temptation to scream, and in screaming to obscure both drama and the issues. For example, Dalton Trumbo's *Johnny Got His Gun* is a film about the same war, whose subject is so fanciful and treatment so heavy-handed that it totally fails to convince. *Paths of Glory* is convincing—maddeningly so. It seethes with indignation, an indignation which grows from Kubrick's skillful treatment of his materials, not from an editorial cloud of anger.

Paths of Glory is shaped by two conflicting forces, with

a man caught in the middle. On the one hand, we have the army officers, especially one arrogant, self-seeking general (George Macready) and his lackeys, who are willing to sacrifice huge numbers of men in an impossible assault which, even if miraculously successful, will have little effect on the course of the war, but which can gain them personal aggrandizement. On the other hand, we have the infantry men, brave and loyal for the most part, whose only real military deficiency is the desire to stay alive if they can. In the middle is Col. Dax (Kirk Douglas), a criminal lawyer in civilian life, who leads the suicide assault and returns to find three of his men, chosen capriciously by their immediate superiors, standing trial for cowardice because their attack failed. It is a thoroughly preposterous policy, yet one, Dax is assured, "quite common in the French army" because "executions [are] a perfect tonic for the entire division."

Quite obviously, such a story has all the makings of a propaganda picture and it is to Kubrick's credit that *Paths of Glory* is not propaganda, but an intensely human and personal film. In later films Kubrick tends to lose track of people as people —the characters in *Dr. Strangelove* are marvelous, but they are caricatures; his *2001* astronauts are intentionally impersonal; and the characters in *A Clockwork Orange* are stylized to be vicious, banal, and stupid. But in *Paths of Glory* the audience is held at little distance from the screen people. Its involving power stems directly from the audience's involvement with a number of characters, not, as in Kubrick's later film's, from the director's arresting vision or technical skills, or from particularly entertaining performances like those of Peter Sellers and George C. Scott in *Lolita* and *Dr. Strangelove*.

Much is made of Kubrick's technical genius, and, especially in the light of the nearly actorless *2001*, it is easy to forget that in films like *Paths of Glory* and *Lolita* he gets tremendous acting from a wide variety of actors and actresses, including some who have performed badly or listlessly in other films. He explains his technique in a *Newsweek* interview with Paul D. Zimmerman, saying, "To get the best possible performances from an actor you have to give him good dramatic ideas."[1]

[1] Zimmerman, p. 32.

18

If it were that easy, anybody with sure dramatic instincts would get consistently good acting from film actors. But over the last fifteen years few American film directors have gotten as many good performances, in so many films, as has Kubrick. Kirk Douglas in *Paths of Glory* is an instance. Douglas is a solid if often dull actor who has given a great many unexciting performances in bad westerns and dull dramas. In this film, however, he is positively fascinating as a man who must lead men to their deaths well aware of, in fact scandalized by, the folly of his task. His romantic motivation for leading the attack—he must do so or lose his command, and he does not want to be separated from his men—seems a bit far-fetched, but his dedication to justice, even in a military setting where, to use Robert Sherril's phrase, "military justice is to justice what military music is to music" is entirely believable. The split role Col. Dax must play as an officer in an army where the officers all seem to be rats and as soldier-lawyer and defender of the rights of man is delicate, but Douglas handles it with grace. Admittedly, his presence as the only lion in a pack of jackals strains credibility a bit, but in this film about one of the cruelest wars ever fought, we are rather eager to believe that most everybody in charge of fighting it was a scoundrel, and at the same time to be reassured in our belief in humanity at finding one decent man among them.

The performances by the three court-martialed soldiers are particularly good. Ralph Meeker plays a tough and competent corporal who is chosen for execution because he knows his superior has murdered one of his own men. Joseph Turkel is a short wiry man who reacts violently to the injustice of his fate. Most striking of the three is Timothy Carey (the horse killer in *The Killing*). He is a tall, sad-faced, slightly simple fellow, chosen for execution because his commander thinks him a "social undesirable." His face is incredibly mobile and reflects an unsoldierly gentleness and innocence. His awkward movement—he seems all arms and legs—and too short uniform accentuate his vulnerability. Of the three victims, he is the most confused and shaken by his plight, and he goes whimpering to the firing squad like a basset hound pup.

19

The execution is staged with the precision and attention to detail that mark all of Kubrick's work. Meeker walks proud and angry through the interminable line of watching soldiers. Carey stumbles along, furiously working a rosary and sobbing. Turkel, whose head Meeker has cracked open in a fight the night before, is carried unconscious on a stretcher. The palace which the generals are using for headquarters stands in the background, and on either side of the procession stand the grim troops. We are not spared a moment of the spectacle, and as the three posts grow larger and larger in the foreground of the long tracking shot, one waits for some sort of miraculous deliverance that never comes. Relentlessly, the drama plays itself out and the three, with Turkel strapped to his stretcher and then to a pole, are blessed by a priest and shot. Macready remarks to Adolphe Menjou (his immediate superior) as the generals breakfast afterwards, "The men died wonderfully. There's always that chance that one of them will do something that will leave a bad taste in everyone's mouth."

Another powerful sequence in *Paths of Glory* is the court martial. It is set in a huge, elegant, baroque hall, in a palace where every footstep and word echoes back and forth a dozen times. Immediately one recognizes the contrast between the opulence of the general's quarters and the sludge and grime of the trenches. Macready sits smugly as the trial begins, and the five judges loaf at their massive desk, bored by the proceedings. The prosecutor makes an absurd, sabre-rattling, flag-waving speech and quickly establishes that none of the three men on trial for cowardice reached the German lines. When Douglas attempts to construct a defense he quickly learns what military justice is all about; anything pertinent to the defense is ruled out of order. When he tries to establish his men's bravery in past battles, he is reminded that the accused are "not being tried for their past bravery, but for their recent cowardice." When he suggests that the attack the men were ordered to make was impossible, the court martial president replies, with perfect logic, that "if it were impossible, the only proof would be their dead bodies lying in the trenches."

Douglas's predicament is one in which every Kubrick main

character sooner or later finds himself. He is trapped in an impossible situation. It is not that he isn't a good, intelligent, resourceful man—he is all three—but that the forces lined up against him are insuperable. In *Paths of Glory* the forces are social. In later Kubrick films (*Dr. Strangelove, 2001*) they will become mechanistic. But in either case we see Kubrick's view of man coming out clearly—in most situations man is inadequate. Men who get mixed up in big things like wars, slave revolts, scandalous romances, and space flights are annihilated. In Douglas's case the situation is particularly ironic since Adolphe Menjou believes that Douglas is cleverly trying to destroy George Macready with a scandal in order to take over Macready's command, when in fact he is merely trying to save the lives of three soldiers.

One scene comes especially to mind. Calmly and kindly he explains the court martial proceedings to the three accused men in the cellar room where they are confined. He is all concerned business, trying to do his efficient best when it is totally obvious to us, and must be to him, that anything he does will be futile. Douglas's rather stolid acting style works well here. Only men who are too stupid (Slim Pickens in *Dr. Strangelove*) or mechanical (Keir Dullea in *2001*) to realize what's happening to them, or who possess incredible self-control, can keep from cracking up in a Kubrick movie, and Douglas exemplifies the self-controlled type.

We see this pessimistic view of the universe very clearly in two short incidental scenes. One involves th three convicted men on the night before their execution. One of the men suggests that a cockroach has more control over its destiny than they do—it will be alive the next morning and they will not. Timothy Carey immediately crushes it, and grins triumphantly. It is a hollow triumph, of course. The cockroach is no better off than they—but on the other hand, they are no better off than it. They snuff the cockroach, tomorrow the generals will snuff them. The other such scene is one of the few humorous moments in *Paths of Glory*. Two soldiers discuss which parts of their bodies they would like least to be shot in, and which weapons scare them most, deciding they are not afraid of dying, merely of getting hurt. The practical relevance of the conversation is null. Neither will have anything to say about where they get shot, and if the enemy doesn't get them, their own generals will. A special irony has Joseph Turkel participating in the discussion, and when he faces the prospect of a firing squad—certainly as painless a way to die as most—he finds that he is not merely afraid of getting hurt.

This theme of futility is reinforced by the visual imagery of the film, especially in the brief battle scenes. The objective of the ill-fated attack is called appropriately "The Anthill," and, as we noted earlier, Douglas and his soldiers do look very much like ants scurrying frantically across the war-mangled no-man's-land. Impersonally, bombs and shells smash them down one by one, like the tread of so many heedless feet. The insect motif is hardly accidental. It also comes up when Carey crushes the cockroach. In Kubrick's films men are very often treated as insects. The pre-battle scenes in *Spartacus*, with the camera scanning huge crawling masses of humanity from above, give the same impression, and the scenes in *2001* of tiny humans working busily behind the windows in huge labyrinthian space stations and vehicles remind one very much of the activity in an ant farm. When questioned in a *Playboy* interview about the possibility of extraterrestrial life contacting earth, Kubrick verbalized the insect metaphor:

> If an intelligent ant suddenly traced a message in the sand at my feet reading, "I am sentient; let's talk things over," I doubt very much that I would rush to grind him under my heel.[2]

The court martial sequence visually enforces the isolation and helplessness of the men, as the hugeness of the room dwarfs them, sitting isolated and alone, separated from observing officers, who sit comfortably together in elegant chairs, and separated from the raised table of the judges. The chilling track toward the stakes in the execution sequence also emphasizes inevitable and impersonal doom.

Despite its determinism and the dehumanization it pictures, this—except for *Spartacus*, which Kubrick did not write—is

[2] Kubrick, quoted by *Playboy*, in Agel, *The Making of Kubrick's 2001*, p. 333.

certainly Kubrick's most "liberal" film. No matter how much he may claim to hate war and violence personally, this is the only Kubrick film in which we get a clear commentary on the proceedings. It is also—again except for *Spartacus*—the most humorless of his pictures. Every other film is in some sense comic, even if brutally and darkly so. The dominant emotions in *Paths of Glory* are outrage and concern. The liberality of the film is reinforced at the end by a potentially corny, but hauntingly effective, scene in which a frail, scared German girl (Susanne Christian—actually Kubrick's wife Christiane) sings for the French soldiers who are about to return to the front. In a series of shots of the soldiers' touchingly expressive and individual faces, Kubrick closes *Paths of Glory* pleading for the humanness of each individual—a humanness which everything in his cinema world is determined to destroy. At this point at least, Kubrick has not learned to stop worrying and to love horrible things.

* * *

Spartacus is the least personal of Kubrick's films for the simple reason that it is the only one which he did not write. In fact, he did not even take part in it until the film had been in production for a week and Kirk Douglas hired him to take over as director for Anthony Mann, who had been fired.

The script for *Spartacus*, based upon the novel by Howard Fast, was written by Dalton Trumbo. Trumbo was one of the famous "Hollywood Ten" who had had the courage to stand up to the House Un-American Activities Committee in 1947 during that august body's investigation of Communist infiltration in the American movie industry. He and nine others were blacklisted for their pains, and for years after that the work Trumbo did in Hollywood was pseudonymous. *Spartacus* was the first movie after the HUAC hearings for which he received screen credit. His political history, of course, commands admiration, but his work hardly does. He is at heart a propagandist, and not a very good one at that. So while *Spartacus* tells a good story and has its moments, particularly in dialogues between Charles Laughton and Peter Ustinov, it is overlong and speechified, given to political harangues, oversimplification, and plain corn. Still, *Spartacus* is a good cut better than most Roman spectaculars, and for that Kubrick is primarily responsible.

In theme and subject *Spartacus* is very much like *Paths of Glory*, although the spectacular ($12,000,000) treatment differs greatly from the low-budget style of its predecessor. It is about the Roman slave revolt of 71 B.C. led by a slave named Spartacus, to this day an historically enigmatic figure. He is heavily romanticized in this film version—the dissension which plagued his slave army and eventually led to his defeat is never even hinted at. Kirk Douglas plays Spartacus, but he isn't nearly as effective as he is in *Paths of Glory*. His performance is good in the gladiator-school sequences but bland after that. The really good performances in this film about a slave revolt are all by the patricians: Laurence Olivier as Crassus, Charles Laughton as Gracchus, and Peter Ustinov (an academy award winner) as Batiatus, are all witty and eloquent.

The best moments are those which are most completely visual—the action and crowd scenes. The long overhead shot of Spartacus' undisciplined horde confronting the Roman phalanxes is absolutely stunning. So are the gladiatorial contests, although they raise a disturbing question. In *Spartacus*, which is about the inhumanity of slavery and the degradation of human combat, both for combatants and observers, the combat is one of the most exciting, enjoyable parts. Kubrick, intentionally or otherwise, is playing a bit of a nasty trick on his audience, making them thrill to the degradation. In fact, Kubrick seems to be enjoying the fights a great deal himself.

The mass sequences of slaves flocking to join Spartacus' growing army are very effective. As in *Paths of Glory*, Kubrick risks sentimentality with close-ups of the faces of the hardworking, honest, recently liberated common folk, and at times, such as in his repeated return to a too endearing pair of seventy-year-old lovebirds, the treatment is bathetic; generally it is powerful though, especially in Spartacus' midnight tour of his camp before the final battle, a scene reminiscent of Kirk Douglas's walk through the trenches to inspect his troops in *Paths of Glory*. At least in one place we see the more typical Kubrick vision: a dwarf and a dachshund dance together. Somehow, this seems more typical of a slave army than all the bliss, brotherhood, and lovingness.

The Kubrick touch is also evident when two beautiful, if overdressed and bloodthirsty, lady patricians come to the gladiator school and cheerfully pick out the men who will entertain them by trying to kill each other. At another point, as the gladiators are introduced to the school, they are told that they will be trained to perform before "ladies and gentlemen of quality—those who appreciate a good kill."

The only strong dialogue in *Spartacus* is between Ustinov and Laughton. Trumbo manages to avoid using them as mouthpieces for propaganda, and the two develop a rhythm between themselves, a witty, slightly bored, wry pattern of conversation. Both of them fat and lecherous, in one very funny scene they discuss their corpulence and tastes in women with ironic gusto. Unfortunately, *Spartacus* is three hours of movie and only about sixty minutes of high spots like those.

Many of *Spartacus'* problems are related to things over which Kubrick had no control. The screaming, rhetorical dialogue is not only annoying, but at times actually ruins what might have been very good scenes. Spartacus first meets his love, Varinia (Jean Simmons), at the gladiator school where she is a slave and a prostitute. When she is thrown into his cell one night, they play a touching scene. Having worked in the mines all his life, he has never made love to a woman, and he approaches her cautiously, fingering the shoulder of her tunic and awkwardly telling her he is a virgin. She is gorgeous and sensitive (a bit unbelievably so, since she does kitchen work by day and is thrown to the gladiators by night) and the scene has poignancy. Almost immediately, however, Douglas launches into a melodramatic spiel about how he is not an animal and she replies in kind. None of the verbiage is the least bit necessary—the brief touch between the two demonstrates both their biological and emotional humanity.

Despite the fact that it is not exclusively his movie, *Spartacus* is of a piece with Kubrick's other work. The class theme, which comes through most clearly in *Paths of Glory* but is

25

certainly present in other Kubrick films as well, is obvious in a film about slaves and their masters. As important, and even more typical, is the picture of a man in the middle of something a whole lot bigger than himself. Kubrick's Spartacus is a good man, certainly the most heroic in any Kubrick film, but in the end history does him in and crucifies him. The fact that his infant son lives after him is so much melodrama, and in view of Spartacus' staggering failure, of no consequence. In fact, the failure of the slave revolt is bleakly ironic. Not only has Spartacus not freed any slaves who are still alive, he has undoubtedly hardened the lot of other slaves to come. Historically, human slavery outlives Spartacus by a couple of millennia.

True, *Spartacus* is a testimonial to the human spirit, but it is also a commentary on the futility of great enterprises. It is not stretching the point to note that Crassus, the final victor in this film, will be defeated and slain in a battle against Parthia, eighteen years later. And another character in the film, a young man named Julius Caesar (John Gavin), eventually fulfills Crassus' dreams of dictatorship over Rome, only to be stabbed to death in the Senate.

3

LOLITA

The thing that seems to have unnerved critics the most about Kubrick's adaptation of Vladimir Nabokov's *Lolita*, when it was released in 1962, was that it was not like the celebrated novel. This, all the more mystifying because Nabokov himself wrote the screenplay. Stanley Kauffmann commented, "It is clear that Nabokov respects the novel. It is equally clear that he does not respect the film—at least as it is used in America."[1] Actually, what happened was that Nabokov supplied Kubrick with an unfilmable script which the director and producer James Harris rewrote in a thirty-day marathon.[2]

Since the novel *Lolita* is one of the most important in contemporary American literature, and since some of the least sensible criticism of this film has come from those who expected it to be more or less like the book, it is worth considering at the outset the changes Kubrick made in translating novel to film.

The most obvious change is that Sue Lyon, who plays Lolita in the film, is not Nabokov's twelve-year-old, 27-23-29, four-foot nine-inch tall, seventy-eight pound nymphet. Miss Lyon was fourteen years old at the time the film was shot, but looks a well-developed seventeen. Because of this, Humbert Humbert's desire for her comes off as ordinary lust quite unlike the elaborately conceived and described perversion which possesses Nabokov's Humbert. That there was simply no other way to make the film seems to have escaped critics at the

[1] Kauffmann, *"Lolita,"* p. 112. [2] Zimmerman, p. 32.

time. Industry censorship would certainly not have permitted a film about the debauching and debaucheries of a grade-schooler, and finding an actress to play *that* part would have been all but impossible. In addition, the thoroughly internal novel makes Humbert's passion clear and believable only by digging deeply into his mind, a difficult task in a movie.

The most important difference between book and film—even more important than the aging of Lolita—stems directly from the latter problem. Nabokov's novel has as its main character the narrator Humbert. In the no longer internalized film, he shares that position with Clare Quilty, the diabolical playwright, an ever present, but only shadowy, figure in the novel. Humbert, played by James Mason, is on screen most of the time, and he is still the film's center of consciousness, but as the film develops, it is Quilty (Peter Sellers) whose motives and actions become the most interesting. Whereas Nabokov introduces us to Quilty through an innocent enough chance reference in a Who's Who of the theater, and a cigarette advertisement, Kubrick brings him on front and center at a dance in Ramsdale, Lolita's home town. Quilty's scene with Humbert at the Enchanted Hunters Hotel is lengthened considerably in the film, and it is Quilty, disguised as the horrific psychiatrist Dr. Zempf, not the novel's matronly school superintendent, Pratt, who talks Humbert into letting Lolita participate in the school play in Beardsley.

Lolita's mother, Charlotte Haze, the story's fourth important character, and for a short while Humbert's wife, is also changed from novel to film. In the novel, seen through Humbert's eyes, Charlotte is a pretentious, "cultured," middle-class dolt, with "quite simple not unattractive features of a type that may be defined as a weak solution of Marlene Dietrich."[3] Shelley Winters' film Charlotte is a burlesque of the original—an incredible culture-vulture, chairwoman of a Great Books Committee, a connoisseur of reproductions, crass and forward as a suitor, schmaltzy and possessive as a wife, and proud of being part of a "culturally...very advanced group. We're very progressive intellectually," she tells Humbert about Ramsdale society.

[3] Nabokov, *Lolita,* p. 36.

Furthermore, Lolita is not the only character to change a great deal physically. Nabokov's Humbert boasts of his brooding good looks: "I was and still am, despite *mes malheurs*, an exceptionally handsome male; slow-moving, tall, with soft dark hair and a gloomy but all the more seductive cast of demeanor."[4] As played by Mason he is pug-nosed and pasty-faced. Quilty, whom the novel describes only vaguely as pudgy and bald, is more rodent-like in Sellers' hands. Sellers is not slim, but somehow he comes off small and weasely before Kubrick's cameras.

But for all these changes in plot, theme, and visual description, Kubrick's film is basically the same story as the novel. Nabokov states in his Afterword to the novel that

> As far as I can recall, the initial shiver of inspiration was somehow prompted by a newspaper story about an ape in the Jardindes Plantes who, after months of coaxing by a scientist, produced the first drawing ever charcoaled by an animal: this sketch showed the bars of the poor creature's cage.[5]

Both movie and book are the record of an imprisoning obsession, although Humbert's obsession is more conventional in the film than in the novel.

One of the best things about the film is its portrayal of the relationship between Humbert and Charlotte. Shelley Winters, killed a third of the way into the film, is around too briefly, but while there she is terrific—her character is a burlesque, but through sheer force of will and talent she makes it a believable, thoroughly enjoyable, burlesque. Constantly aflutter, cigarette holder in hand, she turns genteel Humbert's quest for bliss in her home into a purgatorial, if not hellish, experience. He laughs about her in his journal, but she gives him little amusement or peace face-to-face. The scene in which she tries to teach him to dance is extremely funny. He protests he cannot dance—he has no sense of rhythm—but she locks a vice-grip on him and swings him around, all the while growing more bubbly amorous. By the end of the scene, he who could not dance is prancing to and fro, desperately fleeing her clutches while she clings to him, protesting her passionate nature and the unhappiness of her sexual deprivation as a widow. She

4 Nabokov, p. 26.   5 Nabokov, pp. 282-283.

continues the clutching act after their marriage, mercilessly pursuing him from bedroom to bathroom to study.

In those early home scenes Kubrick pictures well the simultaneously sad and hilarious Humbert-Charlotte-Lolita triangle. In one scene Humbert sits between the two at a drive-in horror movie and each grabs one of his knees and hands in fright. Gingerly he extricates himself from Charlotte and tenderly cradles Lo's terrified fingers with both his hands. In another scene, Lolita retires for the night, pecking her mother's cheek, and lingering at Humbert's. These early scenes turn out to be the high points of the film—except for the times when Sellers appears, it never regains its pace, poignancy, and nasty humor. One of the reasons for that is probably Shelley Winters. Both Mason and Lyon are strong actors while playing against her. But once she leaves the scene they are only adequate in too many instances.

Peter Sellers turns in a wonderful performance as Quilty. In *Dr. Strangelove* he plays three different roles—in *Lolita* he plays a character who himself impersonates three different people—a nosy policeman at the Enchanted Hunters, Dr. Zempf, and a telephone caller who plagues Humbert while Lolita is in the hospital in a small Western town. It's a little difficult to know what to say about him in this film—he is so versatile and so perfect. Despite the fact that we see him on screen a good deal more than we read about him in the novel, he still manages to be a shadowy presence, partly because of the way Kubrick photographs him. The first time Quilty confronts Humbert at the Enchanted Hunters they are on a dimly lit porch and the prey doesn't even notice the hunter until he begins a conversation on the pretext that Humbert looks like a "normal-type guy" with whom he would like to have "a normal-type chat." As he begins to ask about Lolita he keeps returning to Humbert's "normality," and by the end of his prying, insinuating conversation, being "normal" seems like some sort of perversion.

The problem with the film *Lolita* is certainly not the emphasis of the script, or changes made from the novel. Nor is it Sue Lyon, who, if she does not radiate Nabokov's "nymphetness" from the screen, does possess convincing sullen adolescent sexuality. Rather, *Lolita's* greatest weaknesses are problems which Kubrick could either have avoided easily, or which stem from his attempts to do things which he has never done very well in any of his films.

In the first place, surprising as this is for a man who made two such tightly edited and carefully structured films as *The Killing* and *Paths of Glory*, *Lolita* is overlong, dragged-out. The cuts are mostly fade-in, fade-outs, when what is needed is fast cutting to speed up the tempo. Furthermore, it is not so much that specific scenes are too long (although some, like the dance scene at the gym and Humbert's anxious moments trying to lose the car that is tailing him, definitely are), but that practically all of them contain things which might better have been cut for the sake of pacing the film as a whole.

The film's oppressive quality, growing largely from Humbert's tyrannical misuse of Lolita and the awareness that fate, in the form of Quilty, is closing in on him, is necessary to the idea of the film—that of the caged man—and conveyed well, but it is not enough to sustain the last ninety minutes by itself. Except for the points where Sellers comes on the scene, the oppression is about all there is to it. Either humor or a touch of eroticism would have provided necessary variety in tone—humor is less and less evident as the film progresses, and, ostensibly fearing censorship, Kubrick makes only a couple of brief stabs at eroticism in the entire film. One effective attempt is the toe-painting episode in the credit sequence and the other is in the Enchanted Hunters, when Lolita seduces Humbert. There are two versions of that scene: one, less frequently shown, has Lo making veiled references to games she played with boys at summer camp, before a fade-out; a second has her merely whispering the name of one such game to a wide-eyed Humbert as the scene fades.

Kubrick explains:

> Naturally, I regret that the film could not be more erotic. The eroticism...serves a very important purpose in the book, which was lacking in the film: it obscured any hint that Humbert loved Lolita....It was very important to delay an awareness of his love

until the end of the story. I'm afraid that this was all too obvious in the film.[6]

That is astute criticism, but what it ignores is the fact that Kubrick has had few erotic moments in any of his films—including the X-rated *A Clockwork Orange*, which for all its sex and violence is certainly not erotic. Some directors (Truffaut, Claude Chabrol, and Eric Rohmer come to mind) can handle eroticism in a very nongraphic manner, and such a treatment, were Kubrick capable of it, would have added depth and focus to the film. But after nine feature films we can pretty safely assume that this is one of Kubrick's limitations as a director.

This limitation seems to be a product of his reluctance to deal with characters on an emotional human level. As we have noted, some critics, especially Alexander Walker, have made a great deal of Kubrick's love of chess and see chess motifs in many of his films. The central point of such criticism is that Kubrick films picture a mechanistic universe. In that universe people tend to get obscured as people. They become thugs going through their paces in *The Killing*, or generals outflanking each other and using their men as pawns in *Paths of Glory*. In *Paths of Glory*, Kubrick gets as close as he ever does to getting inside his characters, especially Col. Dax and the condemned soldiers. In *Dr. Strangelove* the humans are at the mercy of machines—they have to learn to love the bomb —and in *2001* the machines—notably the HAL 9000 computer—are actually the main characters of the film. In *A Clockwork Orange* we are back to people again, but except for Alex they are either mindless brutes, lobotomized dodos like Alex's parents and the prison guard, or satirical cartoon politicians. Even Alex, for all his love of Beethoven, is hardly what one would call a sensitive human being.

This is a problem in *Lolita*. Nabokov (himself a chess lover—one of his novels, *The Defense*, is structurally based upon a chess problem) shares Kubrick's feeling for people caught in the clutches of an impersonal and, it would seem, intentionally hostile universe. The difference between Nabokov and Kubrick is that Nabokov seems to treat characters, espe-

[6] Kubrick, quoted by Walker, p. 29.

cially Humbert, with a little more respect. Often tender, frightfully vulnerable, and usually confused, he is the most human character in the film, but in Kubrick's mechanistic universe he seems a good deal less noble than in Nabokov's. In the final chapters of *Lolita*, Nabokov exposes not only Humbert but also Charlotte and Lolita as complicated pieces of humanity. Kubrick's Humbert is a bewildered fool at the mercy of Quilty, his Charlotte a caricatured pseudo-sophisticate, and his Lolita a sexy, but shallow, teenage bitch. In this light it is no wonder that Quilty, really only a vague presence in the novel, becomes the most interesting character in the film—the dramatic but not quite human embodiment of that nasty whatever-it-is that the novel's Humbert calls "McFate."

Not to say that *Lolita* does not show flashes, long flashes, of brilliance. It's simply that in this film about people, one misses a little human concern. Without it, *Lolita* becomes tedious.

4

DR. STRANGELOVE, OR HOW I
LEARNED TO STOP WORRYING
AND LOVE THE BOMB

Whatever problems Kubrick might have had with pace and structure in *Spartacus* and *Lolita*, he certainly has none in *Dr. Strangelove*. As in *Paths of Glory*, his material is well in hand—the film is a marvel of fast pace and precise editing. And here Kubrick's material is perfectly suited to his fascination with machines, his love of a game-type structure, and his misanthropy.

The film is a bomb-comedy in which, ironically, systems designed to keep man from destroying himself, prevent him from saving himself from destruction. The desperate humans blunder about, hopelessly inadequate against the entanglements of their technology and their political ideologies. The politicians and soldiers in this film are caricatures, and the effect is that of an exquisite extended political cartoon—we do not really believe in those men, but we certainly do believe in the people they are drawn from. Furthermore, it is impossible, thanks to the sets meticulously designed by Kubrick and his Production Designer Ken Adam and thanks to the implacable logic of the film's chain of events, to doubt the reality of the situation. Perhaps the greatest triumph of *Dr. Strangelove* is that for all its overdrawn zaniness, it is not a thoroughly preposterous movie. In fact, one leaves it with the notion that nuclear annihilation is not only possible, but more or less likely. It is a tribute to Kubrick's dark humor that we laugh our way to destruction in his movie, unsoothed by the laughter, but tingling from the delicious horror of seeing our worst fears about the destiny of mankind confirmed on the screen. It is not exactly a pleasant experience, but there is a sense of relief that the unspeakable has been said and that, our fears confirmed, they are at least out in the open, not back in the deep dark recesses of our skulls.

One of the reasons *Dr. Strangelove* works so well is that for all the absurdity of its characters, they are surrounded by a realism which makes their situation seem very rational even if *they* are not. The design of the interior of the SAC bomber is an example of this realism. Kubrick had not inspected a jet before working on his design, but the forboding, unending banks of instrument panels look absolutely right technically, and thematically they reinforce the idea of men, in this case the hapless crew of the bomber, dwarfed and oppressed by technology. The contrast between the mad major (King) Kong (Slim Pickens), with his Texas drawl, his inane, battle-happy rah-rahism ("Here we go! Nuclear combat, toe to toe with the Rooskies!"), and his Stetson combat hat, and on the other hand the looming dials and gadgets is both hilarious and chilling. As he begins his attack speech, he tells his men, "I reckon you wouldn't even be human beings if you didn't have some pretty strong feelings about nuclear combat."

We find the same effect in the War Room. The austere circular table, haloed by a bank of lights and walled by blinking maps and dials, is perfect, even beautiful in a ghastly, apocalyptic sort of way. Beneath its structural magnificence labor some of the strangest national leaders one could ever hope to meet. Foremost among them President Merkin Muffley (Peter Sellers), the sanest man in the room and thus a sort of weirdo in his sanity; Gen. Buck Turgidson (George C. Scott), the superpatriotic Air Force Chief of Staff; and Dr. Strangelove (Peter Sellers again), the deformed, ex-Nazi chief consultant to the President on matters of nuclear strategy.

Part of the stark credibility of *Dr. Strangelove* is doubtless created by Kubrick's skillful use of available lighting—light emanating from some actual light in the set—especially in the bomber and the War Room. Always a buff for this sort of lighting, Kubrick has said in an interview with Penelope Houston regarding the filming of *A Clockwork Orange:*

> As far as lighting is concerned, the secret of location lighting is to make sure that the practical lamps that you see in the scene are actually lighting the scene. The convention of film lighting in the past was such that the practical lamps were just props, and although the bulb was on it did nothing actually to light the shot. In this case, I went to a great deal of trouble in selecting useful and interesting looking lamps into which we put photofloods or small quartz lights.[1]

In *A Clockwork Orange* the result is a whiteness whiter than white for the stomp sequence in the writer's house, a sequence which looks for all the world as though there were a battery of floodlamps behind the cameras, but in *Dr. Strangelove* the resultant atmosphere is eerie and shadowed. One feels that he is watching some sort of government documentary. Just as the lighting helps to set a mood which is part of the meaning in *The Killing*, where the conspirators conspire in a dim, smoky room; or in *Paths of Glory*, where the dusky trenches are physically oppressive and the trial hall glares, bathed in sunlight through tall windows; or in *Lolita*, where Quilty's death chamber is gothic and the living room where Humbert and Dr. Zempf chat is dimly lit—so in this film the thematic triumph of Kubrick's lighting skill is that in the bomber one is ever aware of the dials and lights on those instrument panels, and in the War Room one either sees the blackness above the halo, or is haunted by the flashing maps and boards.

In structure, *Dr. Strangelove* alternates between three locations—Burpelson Air Force Base, from which the mad Gen. Ripper launches an American attack against the Soviet Union, the War Room in Washington, D. C., and the bomber *Leper Colony*. The key to the story is that all three locations are cut off from communications with each other because Gen. Ripper has sealed off his base so no one will know what he is doing, because the only way to reach the plane is with a three-letter code prefix which no one but Gen. Ripper knows, and because when the code is finally discovered the shock waves from the detonation of a Russian SAM have destroyed the bomber's message-receiving mechanism. So essential is

[1] Kubrick, quoted by Houston, "Kubrick Country," p. 44.

communication for modern diplomacy and warfare that when it breaks down it is quite literally the end of the world. Frantically, the dizzy mortals scurry about trying to outguess each other with absolutely no knowledge of what the other is doing, let alone thinking. *Dr. Strangelove* too is like a chess game, but a chess game in which each player's pieces are visible only to himself and McFate.

What makes all of this not only bearable, but actually entertaining, is the masterful blend of dark humor and satire which scriptwriters Kubrick, Peter George, and Terry Southern concocted. The basis for the script is the novel *Red Alert* by George, a practiced writer in the apocalyptic vein.

Characters like Gen. Jack D. Ripper are not exactly realistic, but he, for example, surely strikes a responsive chord in anyone who has ever been appalled or amused by fanatical American anti-communism. When he launches into his tirade about fluoridation of water, which he asserts began in 1946, coinciding with the formation of "the post-war communist conspiracy," and is the "most monstrously conceived and dangerous communist plot" because it strikes at the purity of "our precious bodily fluids," we both laugh and shudder—laughing at the sheer absurdity of his mania, and shuddering because somewhere we've read about some real-life American group that said more or less the same thing. "Mandrake," the General asks Sellers (in still another role as Ripper's aide—a British officer participating in an officer-exchange program), "have you ever seen a Russian drink a glass of water?" Naturally not. They, knowing full well about fluoridation, drink only vodka.

Sellers in his Mandrake role is the perfect foil for all of this. Properly British, he struggles to figure out what sort of lunacy is going on around him, and to inject a modicum of sanity into it all. Sitting next to Ripper on a sofa with bullets whistling outside and confused alarms of struggle and flight all around him (the Army has invaded the Air Force Base to get to Gen. Ripper), he asks, "Jack, when did you first develop this theory?"

It was "during the physical act of love," the General replies.

He had experienced "a feeling of loss, a profound sense of emptiness... a loss of essence." Ripper has been able to deal with this threat, however. "Women sense my power, and they seek me out. I do not avoid women. But I deny them my essence."

Throughout all this, Sterling Hayden plays Ripper like one of his characteristic tough-guy hoods. Both in manner and appearance he reminds one of Johnny Clay in *The Killing*. Kubrick's shots of him looming in semi-darkness, jaw jutting forward, cigar clamped, filling the screen, hark back rather precisely to the plotting session in the earlier film. The difference is that this time the man is crazed by a political ideology that is somehow bizarrely related to his sexual hangups, instead of by greed.

Escaping the clutches of this sexual psychopath (Ripper commits suicide, taking the bomber recall code with him to his death), Mandrake runs into another American commander with a few sex problems of his own. Working over a scratch pad left by the late Gen. Ripper, he puzzles out the bomber recall code—some combination of "POE" for "Peace on Earth" and "Purity of Essence"—but in trying to relay it to Washington is confronted by dead telephones and the commander of the conquering army, Col. Bat Guano (Keenan Wynn), who is convinced that the trouble at Burpelson is the result of a "preverts [*sic*] mutiny" led by RAF Group Captain Lionel Mandrake. When Mandrake finally talks Guano into letting him use a phone booth ("If you try any preversions in there I'll blow your head off"), he cannot convince the operator to place a call to President Muffley unless he deposit enough change for the call. Twenty cents short, he convinces Guano to shoot open a Coke machine, but only after being warned that it is private property and that if he doesn't get the President on the phone he will "have to answer to the Coca Cola Company."

The military is further satirized in Kubrick's portrayal of Gen. Buck Turgidson, who is a slightly different sort of lunatic. His mania is not some sort of personal psychosis, but an obsession with the machinery and statistics of nuclear war. With an official-looking notebook entitled "World Targets in Megadeaths" before him, he assures the President that if the United States will follow Gen. Ripper's lead and launch an all-out attack against Russia, it will destroy Soviet air power with only "modest and acceptable" American civilian casualties. He slaps the table and proclaims in delight, "Guaranteed, no more than ten or twenty million dead!" grinning from ear to ear.

When news of the Soviet Doomsday Machine is broken, and Dr. Strangelove explains to the President that it will kill every living thing on earth, Scott listens wide-eyed and exclaims to one of the President's aides, "Gee! I wish we had one of them Doomsday Machines."

After the code has been cracked and except for the damaged *Leper Colony* (which, thanks to the Doomsday Machine, will destroy the world if it drops even one of its bombs) all the bombers return, the President asks Turgidson if *Leper Colony* has a chance to get through. Scott has his finest moment in the film as he gloats over American technical superiority and demonstrates evasive bomber tactics with his own body. Arms spread and body all ago, he concludes with a jowl-shaking bomber roar, "Has he got a chance? Has he got a chance?" and then sags as he realizes what he is saying. Scott's performance is marred only by a bit of exaggerated mugging for the camera. Alexander Walker interprets his action thus:

> Again and again Turgidson is "frozen" in some extraordinary posture, usually resembling that of an ape or jackal, either by having the camera cut away from him in mid-grimace or else by holding the camera on him while the actor petrifies himself into some sub-human attitude. This gives the impression of a gargoyle animated by its own wound-up dementia or a jumping jack-in-the-box of manic impulse, tics, spasms, and reflexes.[2]

Actually the effect is distracting. Turgidson is obviously enough an ape or jackal without mannered posturing. In a film built upon speed and pace, such indulgence slows the action. Scott's frenetic movements and incredible grimaces fit until they are stopped so that we can admire the pose. He is buffoon enough,

[2] Walker, p. 177.

and snapshots of his worst moments are not necessary to underscore his buffoonery.

In contrast to the military madness around him, President Muffley is a tower of sanity. But in *Dr. Strangelove's* topsy-turvy world, sanity is a liability. Consequently, Sellers' low-key, perfectly serious President has some of the funniest moments in the film. Because he is the only rational man in the War Room, we identify with him and start to feel the incredible frustration and desperation that he feels.

His liberality and humaneness are important to the film's thrust. He "will not be the greatest mass murderer since Adolph Hitler," he protests to Gen. Turgidson, but the irony is that by the end he will have presided over the destruction of practically the entire human race. Muffley is both tragic and funny because he tries so hard—he is trying to be a good President, he is trying to keep peace, he is trying to control the military, he is trying to do what's right—it's just that all these people, machines, and ideas keep getting in his way. What he doesn't see, even at the end, is that he is caught in a mad, Kubrickian world where all of those things work together in coordinated malevolence to destroy him and his species. He is a player trying to find a game he wouldn't even know the rules for if he did find it. Everywhere he blunders he is outmaneuvered—he wants to talk to Gen. Ripper, but the General cuts off communication from Burpelson Air Force Base; when the troops get through to Gen. Ripper, he is dead; when the recall code is discovered, one bomber can't receive it because a Russian missile, which was supposed to destroy it, only damaged it; when he tells the Russians the bomber's targets so they can shoot it down, the bomber goes somewhere else; when the bomb door won't open, a highly trained, patriotic pilot opens the doors himself and rides the hydrogen bomb like a bucking bronco to the end of the world. What underscores the desperate humor of the whole situation is that, besides all of those problems, the President must deal with a roomful of crazy people who keep pushing him into crazy situations.

While the world goes to oblivion, he must break up a fight between Turgidson and Ambassador de Sadesky, who, complete with matchbox camera, engages in a little extracurricular espionage. "Gentlemen," admonishes Muffley, "you can't fight in here! This is the War Room!" Sellers, on the hot line, trying to reason with the drunken Russian Premier Kissoff, whose evening of wenching has been interrupted ("Now then, Dimitri, you know we've always talked about the possibility of something going wrong with the bomb . . . . The BOMB, Dimitri. The *hydrogen* bomb"), is the perfect image of a man whose world is crumbling around him, as it precisely is.

When he analyzes the situation and attempts to initiate action, Muffley is continually confronted by Turgidson's mindless nuclear militarism. Gen. Ripper's only communication to the Pentagon explains his action, concluding, "So let's get going, there's no other choice. God willing, we shall prevail, in peace and freedom from fear and in true health through the purity and essence of our natural fluids." The President concludes, quite correctly, "This man's obviously a psychotic," and Turgidson rejoins, "Well, Mr. President, I'd like to hold off judgment on a thing like that until all the facts are in." When the President asks him about reliability tests which were supposed to prevent the sort of thing that has happened, Turgidson responds, "I don't think it is fair to condemn a whole program for a single slip-up, sir."

Part of the perverse humor of Muffley's situation is the fact that he has, on someone else's good word, approved programs such as the reliability tests and, notably, an emergency provision for base commanders to assume authority if the national chain of command should be disrupted. These are the programs which are directly responsible for his present plight. The point is clear and well taken: As long as militarism and nuclear bombs are around, a liberal, humane, well-meaning, sane President who tries hard is no assurance of peace, or even of survival. *Dr. Strangelove*, with satiric barbs hoisted high, goes straight at John F. Kennedy's notion that militarists were useful on the Joint Chiefs of Staff because "their job was not policy but soldiering, and he admired them as soldiers."[3]

It is in Dr. Strangelove, the most original and bizarre character in the film, that Kubrick's vision of man and nuclear politics

[3] Schlesinger, *A Thousand Days*, p. 912.

is most strikingly displayed. Peter Sellers, in this his third role in the film, talks with the same spooky German accent that he used as Quilty-Zempf in *Lolita*, but in addition he has a wavy shock of blonde hair, a wheelchair, and a black-gloved right hand which jerks, quivers, and attacks him quite apart from his control. An ex-German, presumably an ex-employee of Hitler's, whose German name was Merkwürdigichliebe, he is the evil genius behind the nation's nuclear weapon research and deployment, the man who runs the machines which are running the men in the War Room. It was he who commissioned the Bland Corporation to study the possibility of a Doomsday Machine, an event which—reported in the *New York Times*, though poor President Muffley never read about it—spurred the Russians to develop theirs.

At this point one ought to say a few words about the Doomsday Machine. It is a "simple" device consisting of fifty H-bombs in the hundred-megaton range, jacketed with Cobalt Thorium-G, a particularly nasty radioactive material which, exploded, will produce "a Doomsday shroud, a lethal cloud of radioactivity which will encircle the earth for ninety years." It is triggered automatically when its country is hit by a nuclear bomb, but cannot be set off by any human. As Ambassador de Sadeski explains, "It is not a thing a sane man would do. The Doomsday Machine is designed to trigger itself *automatically!*" It is cheap, and thoroughly frightening—the perfect deterrent. What the Russians have failed to do with theirs is to announce that they have it before putting it into operation. As Dr. Strangelove objects, "The whole point of the Doomsday Machine is lost if you keep it a secret." The whole point is also lost if any human being can defuse it, and thus it is totally beyond human control.

As the Doomsday crisis progresses, it is Strangelove who comes to the fore. As other characters become weaker and more irrational, Strangelove gathers frenzied strength. Sitting darkly in his wheelchair he broods. After Major Kong and his bucking bomb explode into a screen white-out, it is Strangelove whom we see next, posed before those flashing War Room maps. "Mister President," he says with a leer, "I would not rule out the chance to preserve a nucleus of human specimens."

Dr. Strangelove is a gripping movie. One goes through a series of hopes and shattered expectations. From the first scenes of Burpelson Air Force Base preparing for war, through Gen. Turgidson's incredibly funny but at the same time frightening nuclear chauvinism, through Gen. Ripper's mad harangues, through the riotous hotline conversations, through the coke machine telephone call, through the bomber's final bomb run, one's emotions have been blasted thoroughly and one wants merely to relax hopelessly with a stiff drink as President Muffley and Gen. Turgidson finally do. And at this point Peter Sellers grabs the movie and runs with it one more time, and *Dr. Strangelove* explodes in a final spasm of furious energy.

Desperately protecting himself against his murderous gloved hand, Strangelove proffers his suggestion for the salvation of the human race: Gather powerful and fertile men and sexually attractive women in mine shafts thousands of feet deep, and let them live there for a hundred years. Emerging, "they could then work their way back to our present gross national product inside twenty years."

And then all hell breaks loose in the War Room. Gen. Turgidson screams "We must not allow a mine-shaft gap!" and shouts for war against Russia. Dr. Strangelove, battling the arm which keeps giving the "Seig Heil" salute, calls Muffley "*Mein Führer.*" Ambassador de Sadesky produces another camera and goes back to espionage. Strangelove leaps from his wheelchair, presumably, thanks to the total death and destruction before him, a new man, and cries "*Mein Führer*, I can walk!*" Mushroom clouds burst on screen and over the sound track the soft silky voice of Vera Lynn sings sweetly, "We'll meet again, some sunny day."

It is a horrifying and perfect conclusion. Kubrick, with a wonderful sense of pace, piles shock upon shock, and this final absurdity tops them all.

From a logical standpoint *Dr. Strangelove* does not prove much about nuclear war. A prefatory note which the U.S. Air Force requested after the film's initial release assures us that events portrayed in the film could not happen, and the

Air Force is probably right. But, partly because since Vietnam nobody believes anything the military says anymore, and partly because the film succeeds so profoundly on a deeper, emotional level, that prefatory note seems like just one more of the film's nasty jokes. It would be perfectly easy to believe that Kubrick, not the Air Force, engineered its addition. It hurts to give up logic as the chief weapon in the war to prevent nuclear war, but now that the bomb is with us, it seems unlikely that all the logic in the world will make it go away. *Dr. Strangelove* is a polemic, but it is a masterful polemic, and no humane person would argue that it is not a polemic for the right cause, namely the prevention of nuclear war. No totally reliable nuclear deterrent has yet been found—one hesitates to put faith in Doomsday Machines. Perhaps polemical art like *Dr. Strangelove*, which puts the fear of the bomb in us, is as effective a deterrent to nuclear war as any.

Dr. Strangelove is certainly Kubrick's most thoroughly satisfying film. It is not as impressive as the colossal *2001* can be at times, but it is a more unified and intelligent film. Earlier, I noted what seems to me Kubrick's weakness in projecting humanity. Since *Dr. Strangelove* is stylized satire and polemic, that weakness does not hurt the film. Its strengths are the things that Kubrick does best—probably better than anyone else making movies. Its technical precision, its structure, its highly entertaining acting performances, its lighting, marvelously designed sets, and painstaking camera-work, and the facility with which it handles ideas are superb, and are knit together beautifully.

5

2001: A Space Odyssey

Stanley Kubrick made two of the great films of the 1960's. The first is *Dr. Strangelove*, the second, *2001: A Space Odyssey*. Although *2001* is not without flaws and moments of boredom, it is an incredible work of genius—a huge, totally revolutionary movie which may well be as much a milestone in film history as two such acknowledged landmarks as *Birth of a Nation* and *Citizen Kane*.

Because it ignores the literary conventions of plot and structure, *2001* was the subject of critical controversy upon its release. It found favor with viewers who were able to submerge themselves in simply experiencing it, and disfavor with those who expected it to tell a story and say something.

Not that *2001* doesn't both tell a story and say something. It's just that ideas and story-line are orchestrated in a rich symphony of images of prehistory, outer space, and apocalypse which no previous film had even attempted. In a sense *2001* is a religious piece, a scripture of the human race's evolution from ape to man to god, complete with genesis and apocalypse, hymns of praise to the universe, history, and lessons for survival. Even if one does not take Kubrick's religious vision quite as seriously as Kubrick probably does, he cannot help admiring its breadth and grandeur.

The idea for *2001* came from a short story named "The Sentinel," by science fiction writer Arthur Clarke. "The Sentinel" describes the discovery of an artifact from an ancient nonhuman intelligence on the moon. The artifact is apparently meant to be a signal to that civilization, somewhere in the universe, that man has gained the intelligence and technology to reach and explore the moon. Clarke collaborated with Kubrick on the screenplay, and the story has been inflated to include an earlier prehistoric contact with the extraterrestrials, and to show the eventual ultimate contact after the discovery on the moon.

The film begins in an arid desert where a number of creatures, including man-apes, live bleakly from day to day. The spark which jolts ape-man into tool consciousness comes from some unidentified extraterrestrial intelligence in the form of a gray-black monolith which aligns with sun and moon, and wails. Immediately, the heretofore pitiful apes discover that dry bones can be used to kill game, as well as brother apes during territorial disputes. Skipping the ensuing several million years, the film jumps to 2000 A.D., finding Australopithecus in space, worried about the appearance of its old but unrecognized friend, the monolith, on the moon. Again earth, moon, and slab conjoin, again the slab wails, and man takes off for the planet Jupiter, toward which the monolith is sending radio waves. On the way, two astronauts battle a computer for control of their ship. One survives and takes a head-spinning trip through a time warp, landing in a Louis XVI apartment where he finds another monolith and is reincarnated into a godlike heavenly body.

That, of course, is as bare a story-sketch as can possibly be given. The whole thing takes nearly three hours with intermission, and Kubrick has composed dazzling special effects to illustrate the fable.

Superficially, *2001* is quite unlike any of Kubrick's previous movies. Whereas his other films had been dark, both in atmosphere and in humor, demonstrating his basically pessimistic vision, *2001* is brilliantly alight—even the shots of deep blue space are lit by the stars and flashing spacecraft. Kubrick's earlier movies were earthbound things, emphasizing the pettiness and impotence of humanity; *2001* takes on the whole beauty of the universe, with man ostensibly its conqueror.

For all of that, however, man is still the same creature as in other Kubrick films. As pre-man he is hopelessly inept, and only through the push of interested aliens does he advance into intelligence. When he does move forward, his first action is to kill—killing other animals for food to be sure, but also slaughtering his fellows in a war over a waterhole that is ample for all the apes in the neighborhood. The implication is clear and unflattering—"I kill, therefore I am."

In space, the ultimate frontier for man's technology and imagination, men are decidedly unimaginative and ignoble. They no longer bash each other with bone-clubs, but national rivalries prevent the exchange of important scientific information, and aboard the moon is an American base from which Russians are barred when something unusual is discovered there. The American scientists act mechanically, and, unless speaking in technical terms about technical problems, are incapable of any sort of meaningful verbal communication. After Dr. Heywood Floyd (William Sylvester) makes an incredibly lame and generality-ridden speech to his colleagues about the discovery of the monolith on the moon, he is told "You know that was an excellent speech you gave us, Heywood.... It certainly was.... I'm sure it beefed up morale a helluva lot."

It is not only the dullness of these creatures of the twenty-first century that is disturbing—it is their lack of humanity. If the characters of *Dr. Strangelove* were overdrawn caricatures, the characters in *2001* are all too believable technocrats, trained to fulfill specific mechanical functions, but without any show of emotion or personal human attachments. Husbands and wives are separated from each other for long periods of time without any expressed regrets. Astronaut Frank Poole, aboard the *Discovery* mission to Jupiter, listens in boredom to his parents' pre-recorded off-key rendition of "Happy Birthday." The closest things to a display of emotions in the film are Dr. Floyd's ironic smile while reading instructions for the zero-gravity toilet, and Astronaut Dave Bowman's annoyance at an oven which dispenses processed food slightly too hot. The men of 2001 A.D. are no longer savages, but on the other hand they have none of the ennobling attributes of humane man—aesthetic taste, tenderness, a highly active sense of humor, personal loyalty, an appreciation of mystery. Aloft, surrounded by the incredible majesty of the universe, they seem just slightly bored.

Kubrick underscores this deficiency with his awesome pictures of space. While Dr. Floyd talks perfunctorily with his earthbound daughter from a space-station videophone, the earth, a brilliant spectre, rotates outside his window. In the early space scenes the sun peeks over the arc of the earth, which eerily reflects the glow. To the strains of "The Blue Danube" the *Orion* spaceship and space station waltz through a wonderful circular docking maneuver, and the first words spoken in the film are a seemingly pre-recorded "Here you are, sir," from the lips of a uniformed stewardess. Dr. Floyd, faced with talking about the discovery of the first extraterrestrial contact with the human race, can say only, "You guys have come up with something."

In the sense that *2001* is a film of man in search for something bigger than himself, it is a religious work. What is particularly disturbing about it is its view of man. In a way its view of man is even more frightening than that of *Dr. Strangelove*. In *Strangelove* we at least have the anesthetic of laughter to ease the pain of watching our fellow creatures destroy themselves. *2001* has its humorous moments, but its men are neither stupid nor energetic like those of *Dr. Strangelove*—they are frighteningly soulless. The mystery of the universe with which Kubrick is concerned is something they are not even interested in. They are in the middle of the mystery, rubbing elbows with powers infinitely greater than themselves, with gods if you will, and they don't even know it and probably wouldn't care if they did know. They are as uncomprehending of the forces directing and teaching them as insects must be of the intelligence of man. It is no accident that Dave Bowman's mind must be totally blown in the time warp before he can partake of the cup of the cosmos. Man in *2001* is so wrapped up in his own limited knowledge that he cannot find the gods (or God) in his own galactic backyard. They must capture him and take him for a dizzying ride to their universal palaces.

The ironic thing about this disheartening vision of space-age man is that while Kubrick pictures his characters as soulless, devoid of an aesthetic or mystical appreciation of the universe, he himself certainly is not. No one without such an appreciation could possibly have made this visually magnificent film. In his interview with *Playboy*, Kubrick remarks that "the destruction of this planet would have no significance on a cosmic scale."[1] Yet, the very fact that men like himself make movies like *2001*, which communicate the grandeur of creation, makes man important on a cosmic, or any other scale. To extrapolate in ignorance the existence of creatures infinitely superior to man, and then to judge man's cosmic worth on the basis of that extrapolation, is fruitless. Aside from God, in Christian terms a Being who finds man very important, man knows of no creature superior to himself, and thus he *is* the center of his cosmos. That is not only the best judgment he can make on available information, it is the most useful and ennobling. To argue that man's cosmos is too small is valid only insofar as he has stopped trying to expand it, something neither Kubrick, nor his audience, nor any other sensitive person has done.

Jerome Agel, in his McLuhanesque book *The Making of Kubrick's 2001*, has a hundred-page photo documentary on the technical work that went into filming *2001*, and the scale and volume of Kubrick's effort is staggering. From the ape sequence, in which Kubrick uses a front screen projection against extraordinarily reflective material so that the background image reflects against the backdrop but not against the apes, instead of the customary and generally unreal-looking rear projection, to the marvelously realistic models of space machines, Kubrick put millions of dollars and thousands of hours into making his picture look absolutely right. It's as though, given the success of his War Room and bomber interior, he went berserk for design—constructing space stations and space vehicles like a man possessed. Using a complicated process called "Matte," named after the camera used to make the final print, Kubrick grafted films of people working over instrument panels onto films of his models, and as a result we see people working inside the windows of space vehicles that are actually models eight or ten feet long. For example,

[1] Kubrick, quoted by *Playboy*, in Agel, p. 354.

in the scene of the space-station-to-moon ship *Aries* descending into the landing deck of the moon base, three different prints are used; thus a set only fifteen feet deep and a ship only two feet in diameter look absolutely mammoth on the wide screen, because there are tiny humans working behind seemingly huge windows.

Again and again Kubrick achieves the illusion of incredible vastness with amazingly small sets and models. The overview of the Clavius space port on the moon—a gigantic flat dome that divides into eight pie-slice sections which slowly slide underground at their bases, revealing a square of bright lights —fills the screen. Watching it happen, you would hardly suspect that the whole thing is only ten feet in diameter and that the lights are smaller than flashlight bulbs. It is precisely this sense of hugeness that has been lacking in so many other space movies. Never before has a film so thoroughly convinced viewers that they are watching actual space travel. Also, ironically, probably no other film has ever achieved such totally believable effects with such studied artificiality. It is indeed difficult to believe that most of the footage was shot in a studio at Boreham Wood, in the English Countryside. Construction was mostly from scratch—Special Effects Supervisor Douglas Trumbull describes how the space ships were made:

> Basic construction of models was of wood, fiberglass, plexiglass, steel, brass, aluminum. Fine detailing was made up of special heat-forming, plastic-cladding, flexible metal foils of different textures and thicknesses, and of wire, tubing, and thousands of tiny parts carefully selected from hundreds of plastic model kits, ranging from boxcars and battleships to aircraft and Gemini spacecraft. Cameras could get very close to models with no loss of detail or believability.[2]

One of the technical marvels of the *2001* construction was the (this time) lifesize centrifuge which Kubrick built for shooting the interior of the Discovery spacecraft. The living quarters for that trip are inside the centrifuge—a doughnut which spins to simulate earth gravity. The first scene of the journey has Astronaut Frank Poole (Garry Lockwood) running and shadowboxing around its inner circumference. The camera follows him all the way around, twice. It is mounted above him (toward

[2] Trumbull, quoted by Agel, p. 89.

50

the hole of the doughnut) and Lockwood is more or less running in place while the centrifuge turns at about three miles per hour. The effect is so startling that one can't begin to figure out how it was done. Not that one hasn't seen a dozen miraculous things already—pens floating in air, stewardesses walking up circular walls and exiting upside down from the top of the circle, spaceship and space station waltzing together.

In the scene in which Astronaut Poole is clobbered by his own space pod and retrieved by Astronaut Bowman's, a stunt man was used because a dummy did not float right. It required several takes in which he crashed into the retrieval pod at twice the speed indicated on screen (the camera was speeded up to give the proper drifting effect) before the astronaut finally "floated" into the pod's arms. Less than absolute authenticity would not satisfy the director.

Kubrick has been criticized, notably by Pauline Kael, for the impersonality of Poole's death,[3] but such criticism misses the effective conjunction of theme and image here. The thought of being totally cut off and adrift in space is certainly one of the more terrifying of space-age fantasies, and Poole's death —brought on by a machine under the command of a misanthropic computer—is a perfect expression of this fantasy. The fact that the death is terribly impersonal in all that vastness is precisely its horror. Scenes of Poole's cocoon-like corpse somersaulting into space, and then being clumsily retrieved by the triplet of the pod that killed him, reinforce this. Likewise, the computer-murders of the three hibernating astronauts, illustrated on screen by graphs of their life-functions, is as impersonal and frightening as only death in space could be.

The HAL (heuristically programmed algorithmic) 9000 computer, which has control of the technical aspects of the *Discovery* voyage, is one of the chief marvels of *2001*. Programmed to at least ape human emotions, he declares to a television interviewer early in the voyage, "I enjoy working with people." His voice, that of Canadian actor Douglas Rain, is irritatingly unctuous, and as one reviewer suggested, right from the beginning you know he is a fink. HAL's physical appearance, like all the other constructions and sets in *2001*, is absolutely right.

[3] Kael, "Trash, Art, and the Movies," p. 150.

He is a slightly curved set of panels (because of the circular shape of the ship's living quarters), with several television read-out screens and a number of yellow and red eyes strategically placed around the ship. In addition to being able to converse, he can, thanks to those eyes, look at Astronaut Bowman's sketches and read lips. Ironically, programmed to seem emotional, he eventually commits the film's first emotionally motivated action since the apes clubbed each other over the waterhole, deciding to rub out the spaceship's crew and conduct the Jupiter mission himself.

HAL's motivation for murder is one of the more interesting questions about *2001*. The first sign of trouble aboard ship comes when HAL projects the failure of a small instrument in the *Discovery*'s antenna. Since its functioning is essential for maintaining contact with earth, the matter is critical. Meanwhile, HAL's twin 9000 computer on earth projects no failure, and the astronauts are faced with two "infallible" machines in disagreement with each other—a horrifying prospect, since one of them controls not only the mechanical but also the life-functions systems aboard the ship. HAL has an explanation—the contradiction is due to human error. "This sort of thing has come up before," he tells Poole and Bowman. "It has always been attributable to human error." They decide, however, in a furtive conference in a space pod with all its communication systems switched off, to leave the gadget alone, and if it doesn't fail, to pull HAL's plug. The nefarious computer, putting one of its red eyes to use, reads their lips through a window and kills Poole when he goes out. "This mission is too important for me to allow you to jeopardize it," he tells Dave Bowman.

Arthur Clarke, who tends to take a very doctrinal approach to the film, sees HAL as an extension of the tool-consciousness which started mankind (in the case of *2001*, the man-apes) toward humanness. Just as use of the bone-tool-weapon was the start of human civilization, so the computer, as an extension of man, is a giant step in man's evolution:

> The tools the ape-men invented caused them to evolve into their successor, *homo sapiens*. The tool we have invented *is* our suc-

cessor. Biological evolution has given way to a more rapid process —technical evolution. The machine is going to take over.[4]

Clarke is quick to come to HAL's defense.

I personally would like to have seen a rationale for HAL's behavior. It's perfectly understandable, and in fact would have made HAL a very sympathetic character; he had been fouled by those clods at Mission Control [programmed to prevent Poole and Bowman from learning the purpose of their mission]. HAL was indeed correct in attributing his mistaken report to human error.[5]

Clarke's view, however, is not exactly that conveyed by the film. For one thing, it is not at all clear that it is HAL who pushes Dave Bowman into the next step in man's evolution. By the time Bowman hits the time warp, HAL has been turned off, and there really is no indication that all five astronauts would not have done the same thing had HAL behaved perfectly. In terms of theme the importance of the conflict between Bowman and the computer seems not to be that HAL pushes man into his evolutionary leap, but that Bowman must undergo some sort of incredible test, a rite of passage, before his leap forward. Another possibility is that this second extraterrestrial intervention comes, like the first, at a crucial point in man's history. Just as the man-apes had run into a dead end, barely scraping by in the desert, so twenty-first century man has come to a dead end in 2001, losing his soul, and now control of his destiny, to his technology. Perhaps the point of the whole HAL business is that Bowman, in battling HAL and winning, reasserts the integrity of mankind.

No matter how much Clarke may think of HAL as a good guy, the computer definitely comes across as a bad guy in the film. Programmed to simulate emotions, somewhere along the line he seems to have picked up the real thing. The cunning irony—doubtless a product of Kubrick's humor—is that the more human he becomes, the nastier he becomes. He is proud and willful, and when his pride is hurt and his life threatened, he does what any other human being would do: he becomes murderous. It has been pointed out, correctly, that he is the

[4] Clarke, quoted by Agel, p. 117.   [5] Clarke, quoted by Agel, p. 133.

most "human" character in *2001*. True to the Kubrick world-view, he is also the nastiest.

The scene in which Astronaut Bowman shuts him down is one of the most effective in the film. In a glowing red room, Bowman unscrews, one by one, the connections in HAL's memory circuits. Each time he does so, a white translucent slab about the size of a tape cassette slips, almost floats, out of the walls. It is an eerily evocative scene. The red light, the little slabs moving gradually, Bowman's labored breathing, and HAL's becoming less and less quick, panicky as he feels himself "losing his mind," trying to talk Bowman out of it, all add to the scene's weird power. "You're making a big mistake, Dave," HAL pleads, and adds in the film's most wildly humorous understatement, "I realize everything hasn't been quite right with me." As Bowman pulls the plugs, HAL lapses into a spooky, low-key hysteria: "Dave. Stop. Stop. Will you. Stop, Dave. Will you stop, Dave. Stop, Dave. I'm afraid. I'm afraid, Dave. Dave. My mind is going. I can feel it. My mind is going. There is no question about it. I can feel it. I can feel it. I can feel it. I'm afraid." Then HAL begins singing, slowly, like a record winding down on a Vic-trola, "Daisy, Daisy, give me your answer, do. I'm half crazy over the love of you." As HAL dies, the viewer's pain at his death is the best indication of how skillfully Kubrick has created a human character from a machine.

The light show that illuminates Astronaut Bowman's trip through the time warp to his mysterious destination is dazzling. In different scenes, colored lights zip across the screen toward the viewer; nebulae and star whirls ooze and blossom; land-scapes, very much like those flown over by the bomber in *Dr. Strangelove*, appear, but this time colored in iridescent combinations of blue and red, violet and green, turquoise and gold. Dazzling as it is, this sequence was probably one of the easiest to film in *2001*. Water on gasoline, mirrors, color tints, and a slit-screen device which films flashing patterns of abstract paintings, electron microscope photos, and anything else that might look interesting were used, with stylistic indebt-edness to the experimental filmmakers of the early sixties.

The genius of these effects is not that they are difficult or original, but that, after the other wonders of the film, especially that stunning evocation of the sensation of space flight, the viewer is prepared to believe anything. The difference between this light show and most others is that in the others one just watches the marvelous patterns. In *2001* the viewer feels that he really has gone from space to some kind of jump-space. One wonders not how it was done, but where in the universe he is being taken.

2001 does have some problems, not the least of which is its length. Especially as it is shown now, without intermission, the *Discovery* sequence lags. Initially there was an intermission after HAL's lip-reading scene, and the film resumed with Poole going EVA for surgery on the ship's antenna. That ten-minute break helps the pacing tremendously, and it's too bad that it has been eliminated so that theater owners can show the film twice in one night.

Perhaps a bigger difficulty with the film, and this is not really the fault of the film, is the passion its viewers have had for interpretation. Arthur Clarke, especially, has fed this with attempts, after the fact, to explain what *2001* "means." Clarke, especially in the novelization written simultaneously with the screenplay, is at great pains to explain exactly what is happening all the way. The joke going around has been that to understand the film *2001* you must read the book *2001*. In fact, the book is tedious fare, dully written and overintellectualized. The film *2001* succeeds most on the "once-upon-a-spaceman" level—attempts to allegorize precisely get quite dismal. If HAL must stand for something, he becomes much less interesting: we can get much more involved in the "see, there's this spaceman who has a run-in with his computer" aspects of the tale. Nobody—not Kubrick, not Arthur Clarke—knows with any certainty where mankind is going. Taking *2001* as one possible cosmic fantasy is fun—taking it as a serious prophecy is nonsense. Those who look for statements and meanings in this film will be confused. Those who read the novel and find them there should be bored. *2001* is most of all a wonderful picture show about man in space. Kubrick may even want us to ask

"What does it mean?" but a much more interesting and important question is simply "What is going on?" Except for the very end of the picture, which finds Dave Bowman in that mysterious room, answers to the second question are not all that difficult. The morals, allegories, and statements which some viewers have asked for are simply not important. To be sure, the film has implications —man is horrible, man is great; computers are a menace, computers are our descendants; space is magnificent, space is scary; man will not last the next century, man will last forever but in another form. Any and all of these can be inferred, but none of these is the film's meaning. What *2001* "means" is what we see, and what we see is very beautiful and great fun.

6

A Clockwork Orange

A Clockwork Orange is based on Anthony Burgess's novel by the same title. In terms of plot, film and novel are pretty much the same, but Kubrick's vision is a good deal blacker than Burgess's, and the thrust of the film is quite different from that of the novel. The story is set in the not-too-distant future, in an England whose authoritarian government has provided the physical necessities of life for most citizens but has not managed to control the darker aspects of human nature. Thus the society is beset by small gangs of young hooligans who plunder and brutalize at will by night. The story is narrated by Alex, the leader of one such gang. One of the book's most intriguing aspects is the speech of these youngsters, a fetching, and not totally confusing, combination of Cockney slang and Russian translation-transliterations (in the Ballantine edition of the novel, Stanley Hyman has provided a glossary) called NADSAT.

Alex is apprehended one night, and sent to prison for murder. While there, he volunteers for an experimental rehabilitation program, the "Ludovico Treatment," which leaves him incapable of either violence or sex, because he becomes deathly ill at the thought of either. The only problem is that although he is "cured" of extreme antisocial behavior, he is also rendered incapable of moral choice. He has become a "clockwork orange," explained in the novel, though never in the film, as the product of "the attempt to impose upon man, a creature of growth and capable of sweetness, to attempt to impose,

I say, laws and conditions appropriate to a mechanical creature."[1] The novel itself is a Christian parable of the necessity of free will.

Criticizing movies simply because they are not the same as the books they are based on is hardly legitimate in itself, but in this case it is helpful to notice the difference between a superficially similar novel and film. Kubrick has taken an important futuristic novel and without changing much of the plot has markedly changed its emphasis.

One thing he has done is to implant in the film his own negative attitude toward the human race. "Man isn't a noble savage," Kubrick has stated. "He is irrational, brutal, weak, unable to be objective about anything where his own interests are involved... and any attempt to create social institutions to a false view of the nature of man is probably doomed to failure."[2] This may sound Calvinistic Christian, but Calvinism also preaches the possibility of redemption, and even Calvin, wrapped in his own philosophical system, saw that however much he believed in total depravity, there were plenty of people around who were living decent lives and doing good, magnanimous, totally praiseworthy things. In earlier Kubrick films, human beings are often incompetent, or morally impotent, or just plain wicked. Yet some of these earlier characters do show flashes of human charity and good intentions, even if they can't fulfill them. Humbert Humbert is not a monster: for all its perversity, his love for Lolita is more than simple carnality—it is also love. Captain Mandrake and President Muffley are unequal to the furor of madmen and machines, but unlike most of the characters in *Dr. Strangelove* they are not insensitive to the horrors of nuclear war. In *2001*, however, the humans are mechanized—spiritually, morally, and emotionally neutral—dwarfed by their machines and the majesty of the universe, and in *A Clockwork Orange* Kubrick's view of man is even more pessimistic, and more importantly, seems to be turning into a doctrine which controls, rather than simply informs, his art.

[1] Burgess, *A Clockwork Orange,* p. 27.
[2] Kubrick, quoted by Hechinger, "Liberals Should Hate Ideology Behind 'Clockwork Orange'," p. 3-H.

The major difference between the novel and film versions of *A Clockwork Orange* has to do with this view of man. Burgess's Alex is a horrible young man with very few redeeming qualities. He loves music, but in an orgiastic sort of way—he masturbates to Bach and Mozart—and in the novel this is a tribute to the primitive emotional power of great music, not to Alex's good taste. Certainly, Burgess's Alex is no cultured bandit—he and his gang stomp an old bookworm professor (Kubrick changes this character to a derelict in an alley), and destroy priceless books in a library. The Alex of the novel is a witty narrator, but otherwise a sadistic slob. In creating a character like this, Burgess underscores his belief in the importance of free will—even the likes of Alex must have it as human beings. Although the novel's universe is not particularly attractive, Alex does have alternatives. He can choose good or evil and Burgess argues that choosing evil is better, is more human, than being automated to do good.

Kubrick has twisted this vision. To choose between good and evil there must be some good to choose, and Kubrick takes great pains to make every character in the film so ridiculous, so thoroughly unattractive, that the audience can't possibly sympathize with them. He takes pains to make every institution—church, prison, government—totally absurd. This is Kubrickland, where every man is an ignoble savage and every action selfishly motivated. In this context, Alex is the most attractive character since he is the only one who is truly alive. As played by Malcolm McDowell, he has Beethoven, he has the engaging NADSAT lingo, and he has Kubrick's cameras on his side. The focus has been changed, however. Whereas in the novel Alex had a choice between good and evil, in the film he does not. In the film his choice is between banal, stupid, half-hearted evil and flourishing, thorough, spectacular evil. Small wonder we approve his choice.

The great stylistic problem in *A Clockwork Orange,* however, is not that Kubrick has stacked the deck, but that he has done it so clumsily. The people Alex victimizes—and that is just about everybody in the film—are not only banally evil, they are banally conceived. Kubrick has played on just about every conceivable popular social prejudice in creating his supporting cast. We have homosexuals, a Mom and Pop who can't control their child, mindless goons, mindless bureaucrats, a hell-fire and brimstone preacher who sees visions, an effete intellectual, a drunken bum, sexy teeny-boppers, and a health-nut who keeps pop-pornographic art on her walls and a million cats underfoot. Anyone who wants to show us the badness of the world has to be a bit more subtle than that.

Compounding this lack of subtlety is the film's fundamental dishonesty. We sympathize with Alex because he is the most interesting character in the film, and it would seem that Kubrick wants us to make the jump from most interesting to best or most moral. Indeed, a number of critics have made precisely that jump. Paul D. Zimmerman wrote in a *Newsweek* cover-story on Kubrick that "Alex is despicable in what he does, but graced with a wit, energy and demonic imagination that make him superior to any other figure in his world...."[3] Alex is energetic all right, but he is also a psychopath who in any civilized society would be put in an asylum. The other characters in the film are hardly attractive, and a society full of their like would be unpleasant, but on the other hand one would prefer any of them over Alex for a next door neighbor. One wonders how far out of whack values have become when a compulsive sadist and rapist is regarded as superior to caricatured faggots, weak parents, and petty fascists. Alex himself is the ultimate pervert and fascist, and one should certainly question the values of a movie which glorifies him.

A related distasteful element in the film is its pornographic use of violence. In the past few years, especially in America, movies have become progressively more violent. Arthur Penn's *Bonnie and Clyde*, a truly great film, was a watershed in film violence. But as perceptive viewers realized, the horrifying violence in that film worked toward a thematic purpose. Penn's film is about what violence does to its practitioners, and in making Bonnie and Clyde sympathetic (though not whitewashed) characters, he involves his audience with the violence the bandits do and which is done to them. The result

[3] Zimmerman, p. 28.

is a film which thrills the viewer with violence and then turns on him and makes him feel the horrifying brutality of Bonnie and Clyde's own death in a machine-gun ambush—filmed in agonizing slow motion.

But even so excellent a film as *Bonnie and Clyde* has had disturbing effects, which have been largely ignored by those cinema buffs who have recognized the film's great power and beauty. The problem is that not every moviegoer is mature or even sane, and there have been a number of young couples who saw the film (including two youngsters who saw the film the same evening, in the same theater, as this writer first saw it) and then went out on "Bonnie and Clyde"-style criminal binges culminating in murder. Although discussions of the effects of movie violence were heard after the release of that film, those discussions have become less and less frequent. Few people concerned with a form of communication want to see it censored, and objections to violence in movies have come to be regarded as a new sort of Comstockism.

What has developed in the movies is an aesthetic of violence, best seen in another first-rate movie, Sam Peckinpah's *The Wild Bunch*, whose blood-spurting conclusion, in which scores of people are gunned down during the ultimate screen massacre, is truly beautiful, if you can see it in the abstract and remind yourself that those aren't *real* people being killed. Other, less artistic directors have made films like *The Good, the Bad, and the Ugly*, and *Dirty Harry* in which, seemingly, the violence and blood are the movie's basic reason for being.

The violent trend in film is particularly distressing in the light of the Surgeon General's report on televised violence. The report itself was well massaged by the media—the major television networks had a large hand in shaping the committee which researched and wrote the report—but some reporters, notably *Newsweek's* Joseph Morgenstern, plowed through the bureaucratic prose and found the report's basic content quite disturbing:

> Whether by intent or ineptitude the committee misrepresented some of the data, ignored some of it and buried all of it alive in prose that was obviously meant to be unreadable and unread.

The five supporting volumes are still being withheld from the public. Thus far, the news media have accepted the committee's summary as the last word on the research. Beneath the misleading headline "TV Violence Held Unharmful to Youth," The New York Times story stressed contradictions in the Surgeon General's report and, with incomplete quotations, gave the impression that televised violence leads to increased aggressive behavior only in small groups of youngsters.

In fact, the summary says much more than this, and the supporting data says more than the summary. The summary dismisses as unsubstantiated the catharsis theory—that viewing filmed violence allows pent-up emotions to be released harmlessly. While the summary does say that the most direct effects of media violence may occur among children predisposed to violence, it stresses that this violence-prone subgroup may constitute a "small portion or a substantial portion of the total population of young viewers." And an overview of one of the five volumes of supporting research says, in an italicized conclusion, that *"the present entertainment offerings of the television medium may be contributing, in some measure, to the aggressive behavior of many normal children. Such an effect has now been shown in a wide variety of situations."* [4]

That report deals with children—what filmed or televised violence does to adults is anyone's guess, but anyone who has come away from violent entertainment eager to punch someone in the nose has at least a partial, personal, answer to that question.

In *A Clockwork Orange* Kubrick uses orchestrated violence as in *The Wild Bunch*, but his basic intent seems sick. The length and number of beatings administered by Alex and his droogs are excessive, to say the least. What is more, the film, especially the first third, is structured so that the stomping and raping are the high points. Set to beautiful classical music (largely Purcell, Rossini, and Beethoven), Alex's capers are given a specious pretentious dance quality which they simply don't deserve. It is pornography at its worst—the exploitation of perversion to entertain the viewer. In an early scene Kubrick's camera voyeuristically follows as five thugs decked out in Nazi gear (not Alex's gang but a rival one) strip, squeeze,

4 Morgenstern, "The New Violence," p. 66.

and attempt to rape a girl in an old and opulent but battered theater (on stage, of course). It is obvious that Kubrick is enjoying that wagging pink flesh and that the viewer is supposed to enjoy it too. All the Rossini in the world cannot disguise its basically pornographic intent.

The highly touted scene in which Alex stomps a bound and gagged victim (Patrick McGee) while singing and hard-booting through "Singin' in the Rain" seems equally repellent. The lighting looks like that of a football stadium, the contemporary decor is austere, the music is lilting, and the total effect is spare and clinical, but also incredibly vicious. It isn't funny, it isn't really very shocking, it's just plain mean.

When Alex and his droogs creep up to a house in the night, they remind one very much of Charles Manson's family. Ed Sanders, who wrote the book *The Family*, calls it "creepy crawling" and it describes pretty well what Alex and the boys are doing. The apologists for Kubrick suggest that he is exorcising private demons in this movie and that we all ought to come face to face with our own fear of such goings on. But there is a difference between coming face to face with our fear of the bomb as in *Dr. Strangelove*—and being entertained by sadistic brutes creepy-crawling. Besides, Kubrick's treatment of those moments makes it clear that he thinks Alex and the gang are pretty cute. A lot of counter-culture people expected Ed Sanders to find Charlie Manson cute, but he disappointed them. "Some people were expecting a sort of chop chic, but I hate murderers and Satanists. I don't believe in capital punishment, but I really *don't like murderers*."[5] Kubrick, the self-styled prophet of the destiny of the human race, has sold out where Sanders refused to, glorifying the cult of snuff.

To object to such glorification of sadism and violence is not particularly fashionable right now. Yet one does not have to be an advocate of censorship, a prude, or an ignoramus to get tired of it. I suppose that spurting blood and gang-rape and musical stomping can have legitimate aesthetic uses, but

[5] Sanders, quoted in "Backstage with *Esquire*," p. 10.

in current television and movie fare violence has become mindless and a fetish in too many instances. Pauline Kael of *The New Yorker* frames the issue well:

> At the movies, we are gradually being conditioned to accept violence. The directors used to say they were showing us its real face and how ugly it was in order to sensitize us to its horrors. You don't have to be very keen to see that they are now in fact desensitizing us. They are saying that everyone is brutal, and the heroes must be as brutal as the villains or they turn into fools. There seems to be an assumption that if you're offended by movie brutality, you are playing into the hands of the people who want censorship. But this would deny those of us who don't believe in censorship the use of the only counterbalance: the freedom of the press to say that there's anything conceivably damaging in these films—the freedom to analyze their implications.[6]

Andrew Sarris pursues the same line of thought in, ironically enough, the properly leftist *Village Voice*:

> At the moment, I am not particularly concerned about Big Brother clamping electrodes on my skull, nor about the tyranny of Law and Order. What frightens me is the chaos that engulfs us all. I am tired of the cult of violence. I am tired of people smashing other people and things in the name of freedom and self-expression.[7]

Sarris is partially right, I think, but he misses the point that Big Brotherism feeds on chaos and eventually can grow from it. Both Big Brotherism and chaos are real threats to American society. What is desperately necessary is a balance between order and the freedom necessary to live a decent life. Values like those expressed in *A Clockwork Orange* certainly do little to help achieve that balance.

Sarris is quite right in his evaluation of the film's overall impact, however. "Don't take my word for it," he quips. "See *A Clockwork Orange* for yourself and suffer the damnation of boredom."[8] Social and moral objections aside, this may be the film's greatest weakness. It is too long and it is dull. The first third, which deals with Alex's raping and stomping,

---

[6] Kael, "Stanley Strangelove," pp. 52-53.   [8] Sarris, p. 49.
[7] Sarris, "Films in Focus," p. 50.

has the most kinetic excitement, but Kubrick's enchantment with perverse violence makes it offensive. The next third which covers Alex's imprisonment and "rehabilitation" bogs down badly in stale satire of bureaucrats, prison officials, prison fags, and the prison chaplain. This section does have its moments —notably the sequence in which Alex's incapability of violent action is demonstrated to government officials. Here he is tempted by a lithe blonde girl clad only in very slim bikini panties. Alex's natural instinct is to grope, but the treatment has conditioned him to become sickened by even the thought. As he writhes on the floor she pirouettes away—bowing and curtsying winningly to her applauding audience, her breasts bouncing happily. But even this scene is spoiled by Kubrick's insistence that we watch the puritanical chaplain and prison guard ogle her. At this point his obsession with the rottenness of humankind is getting in the way of his usually keen pacing. The last part of the film, which shows Alex's unfortunate return to society, where most of his former victims now victimize him, is just plain not very interesting. Particularly loathsome is the acting of Patrick McGee, as the writer who attempts to kill Alex with Beethoven, another commodity which the Ludovico treatment has made him allergic to.

On the positive side there are some terrific compositions in *A Clockwork Orange*. Kubrick has certainly not lost his eye for taking pictures. The film's initial frames, with Alex clad in his white goon-suit with long false eyelashes on one eye, are startling and promising. Some impressive modern architecture is used in scenes near Alex's apartment, and in the creepy-crawl scenes by the writer's house. And Alex, strapped to a chair, head held in place, wired for nerve impulses, and his eyes held open with metal clamps, in a dark auditorium watching pornographic films during the treatment, makes an arresting sight.

But these bedazzlements are not enough to make the whole movie go. And at other times Kubrick's compositions and direction are self-indulgent, using techniques which are almost precise duplicates of some of the more stunning moments in *2001*. Alex and his droogs beating up the rival gang in the theater use the same quick overhand thrashing method that the recently armed apes do in *2001*. Alex, reasserting his control of the gang, bashes up two rebel droogs in the same fanatic, violent slow motion that the ape leader uses after discovering the club. When Alex dines on spaghetti at the writer's home, the feeding sound effects are the same as those during Keir Dullea's last supper. And at one point, in a quiet hospital room, we even hear that heavy Space Odyssean breathing. Kubrick's other films are notable for their remarkable difference from each other. Here he seems determined to self-consciously add "Kubrick touches," a practice which rather than reinforcing his genius makes one wonder if he has decided to rest on a few tried and true gimmicks.

Kubrick's use of music in *A Clockwork Orange* is clever, but not necessarily brilliant. Using both conventional orchestration and music electronically synthesized by William Carlos, the film offers us some pretty great sounds. But what Kubrick is doing is really a kind of Ludovico treatment in itself. Just as Alex associates the effect of the drugs he is given with the sex and violence he sees during the treatment, and assumes the sex and violence are making him sick, so Kubrick associates what happens on the screen with music and attempts to stir up some exaltation that way. It works best in the film's final scene when Alex is cured of his cure and listens to Beethoven's Ninth, all the while "viddying" himself groping with a luscious blonde "devotchka." It is a powerful conclusion, but most of the power comes from that incredible music, which would make a film of virtually anything seem exciting. The scene is "right," but in a glib, too obvious, sort of way. It sends chills up and down a viewer's spine, but then so does Beethoven's Ninth all by itself, at home on the stereo.

How did Kubrick, who has made great films in the past, make such an undistinguished one this time? Rather obviously, he was as meticulous as ever with *A Clockwork Orange*; its failure is not the result of his not trying. On the contrary, it may be the opposite—that he tried too hard. It is true that too much has been made of Kubrick as the Jewish kid from Brooklyn who never went to college and has been trying ever since to be an intellectual. Yet, in the past few years both his work and his statements in interviews have been taking on an aura of strained profundity. Especially in the *Playboy* interview about *2001*, where Kubrick states that he can't talk about his movie because it is a nonverbal statement and then goes on to make grand verbal statements about the past, present, and future of the universe, and in the Penelope Houston interview about *A Clockwork Orange*, printed in the Dec. 25, 1971, *Saturday Review*, he seems to be going out of his way to be significant. He also seems possessed with the idea of his own undeniable genius, and in *A Clockwork Orange* this leads to a self-indulgent style of filmmaking.

The central problem with *A Clockwork Orange* is Kubrick's *hubris*—his overweening pride in his own skill. He seems to think that when he mocks homosexuals, simpleminded preachers, and ladies who collect cats and erotic art, it will be funny, even though it rarely is when anyone else does it. He seems to think that in his hands a snake nosing the crotch of a pop-pornographic painting of a nude will be clever instead of silly. He probably thinks that loading his film with real, painted, and sculpted genitalia of both sexes is daringly iconoclastic, when in fact the law of diminishing returns applies. *A Clockwork Orange* proves rather conclusively that even a great artist cannot do just anything his heart desires without becoming trite, boring, and sometimes morally offensive.

The great irony is that *A Clockwork Orange* is the first Kubrick film to have gotten a quick and enthusiastic critical bandwagon. In fact, one wonders if the psychology behind the bandwagon is not rooted in precisely the fact that Kubrick's three previous films had all initially received a bad press and are now regarded as greater or lesser masterpieces. Nobody wanted to get stung like that again, and the result has been an uncritical acceptance of anything Kubrick did. Both *Newsweek* and *Saturday Review* ran cover stories which had apparently been planned long before anyone on the magazine saw the film. The cloud of superlatives in each article doesn't mask the fact that the reviewers do little but relate the plot of the film and compliment the lighting, the acting, and Beethoven. Two fortunate exceptions to the wide critical acclaim were Pauline Kael and Andrew Sarris, both of whom wrote analytical and negative reviews.

At this point, then, the trend in Kubrick's work is downhill —since *Dr. Strangelove* Kubrick has picked up some bad habits and an inflated opinion of his talents which are all too evident on screen. Reportedly, his next project will be a film about Napoleon, which he had hoped to make after *2001* was released. The subject, a power-hungry little man who tries to conquer the world, seems quite appropriate. The Kubrick of *Dr. Strangelove* might even make a good film out of it. On the other hand, he must rid himself of those bad habits if he is to make more films that live up to the genius shown in *Paths of Glory, Dr. Strangelove,* and *2001.*

Bibliography

Agel, Jerome, ed. *The Making of Kubrick's 2001.* New York: Signet, 1970.

Alpert, Hollis. "Milk-Plus and Ultra-Violence," *Saturday Review* (Dec. 25, 1971), pp. 40-41, 60.

"Backstage with *Esquire*," *Esquire* (Nov. 1971), pp. 10, 14.

Burgess, Anthony. *A Clockwork Orange.* New York: Ballantine Books, 1965.

Clarke, Arthur. *2001: A Space Odyssey.* New York: Signet, 1968.

George, Peter. Dr. *Strangelove Or: How I Learned to Stop Worrying and Love the Bomb.* New York: Bantam, 1968.

Hechinger, Fred M. "Liberals Should Hate Ideology Behind 'Clockwork Orange'," *Grand Rapids Press* (NY Times News Service) (Feb. 13, 1972), p. 3-H.

Houston, Penelope. "Kubrick Country," *Saturday Review* (Dec. 25, 1971), pp. 42-43.

Kael, Pauline. *"Lolita,"* in *I Lost It at the Movies.* New York: Bantam, 1966, pp. 183-188.

———"Stanley Strangelove," *The New Yorker,* XLVII, 46 (Jan. 1, 1972), 50-53.

———"Trash, Art, and the Movies," *Going Steady.* New York: Bantam, 1971, pp. 105-158.

Kauffmann, Stanley. *"Dr. Strangelove,"* in *A World on Film.* New York: Delta, 1966, pp. 14-19.

———*"Lolita,"* in *A World on Film.* New York: Delta, 1966, pp. 111-113.

———*"Spartacus,"* in *A World on Film.* New York: Delta, 1966, pp. 23-24.

Morgenstern, Joseph. "The New Violence," *Newsweek* (Feb. 14, 1972), pp. 66-69.

Nabokov, Vladimir. *Lolita.* New York: Fawcett Crest, 1955.

Sanders, Ed. *The Family.* New York: E.P. Dutton and Co., Inc., 1971.

Sarris, Andrew. "Films in Focus," *The Village Voice,* XVI, 52 (Dec. 30, 1971), 49-50.

Schlesinger, Arthur M., Jr. *A Thousand Days.* Boston: Houghton Mifflin Company, 1965.

Walker, Alexander. *Stanley Kubrick Directs.* New York: Harcourt Brace Jovanovich, Inc., 1971.

Zimmerman, Paul D. "Kubrick's Brilliant Vision," *Newsweek* (Jan. 3, 1972), pp. 28-33.

Kubrick Filmography

DAY OF THE FIGHT (U.S.A., 1951)
Documentary short on Walter Cartier, middleweight boxer
Director, Photography, Editor, Sound   Stanley Kubrick
Commentary   Douglas Edwards
Time: 16 minutes
Distributor: R.K.O. Radio

FLYING PADRE (U.S.A., 1951)
Documentary short on the Reverend Fred Stadtmueller, Roman
Catholic missionary of a New Mexican parish of 400 square miles
Director, Photography, Editor, Sound   Stanley Kubrick
Time: 9 minutes
Distributor: R.K.O. Radio

FEAR AND DESIRE (U.S.A., 1953; Stanley Kubrick Productions)
Producer   Stanley Kubrick
Director, Photography, Editor   Stanley Kubrick
Script   Howard O. Sackler
Frank Silvera (Mac), Kenneth Harp (Corby), Virginia Leith (the girl),
Paul Mazursky (Sidney), Steve Coit (Fletcher)
Time: 68 minutes
Distributor: Joseph Burstyn

KILLER'S KISS (U.S.A., 1955; Minotaur)
Producers   Stanley Kubrick
                                     Morris Bousel
Director, Photography, Editor   Stanley Kubrick
Script   Stanley Kubrick
                                     Howard O. Sackler
Music   Gerald Fried
Choreography   David Vaughan
Frank Silvera (Vincent Rapallo), Jamie Smith (Davy Gordon), Irene
Kane (Gloria Price), Jerry Jarret (Albert), Iris (Ruth Sobotka), Mike
Dana, Felice Orlandi, Ralph Roberts, Phil Stevenson (hoodlums),
Julius Adelman (owner of mannequin factory), David Vaughan, Alec
Rubin (Conventioneers)
Time: 64 minutes
Distributor: United Artists

THE KILLING (U.S.A., 1956; Harris-Kubrick Productions)
Producer   James B. Harris
Director   Stanley Kubrick
Script   Stanley Kubrick, based on the novel
                             Clean Break, by Lionel White

Additional dialogue	Jim Thompson
Photography	Lucien Ballard
Editor	Betty Steinberg
Art Director	Ruth Sobotka Kubrick
Music	Gerald Fried
Sound	Earl Snyder

Sterling Hayden (Johnny Clay), Jay C. Flippen (Marvin Unger), Marie Windsor (Sherry Peatty), Elisha Cook (George Peatty), Coleen Gray (Fay), Vince Edwards (Val Cannon), Ted de Corsia (Randy Kennan), Joe Sawyer (Mike O'Reilly), Tim Carey (Nikki), Kola Kwariani (Maurice), James Edwards (parking attendant)
Time: 83 minutes
Distributor: United Artists

PATHS OF GLORY (U.S.A., 1957; Harris-Kubrick Productions)
Producer	James B. Harris
Director	Stanley Kubrick
Script	Stanley Kubrick, Calder Willingham, Jim Thompson, based on the novel by Humphrey Cobb
Photography	George Krause
Editor	Eva Kroll
Art Director	Ludwig Reiber
Music	Gerald Fried
Sound	Martin Muller

Kirk Douglas (Colonel Dax), Ralph Meeker (Corporal Paris), Adolphe Menjou (General Broulard), George Macready (General Mireau), Wayne Morris (Lieutenant Roget), Richard Anderson (Major Saint-Auban), Joseph Turkel (Private Arnaud), Timothy Carey (Private Ferol), Peter Capell (Colonel Judge), Susanne Christian (German girl), Bert Freed (Sergeant Boulanger), Emile Meyer (priest), John Stein (Captain Rousseau)
Time: 86 minutes
Distributor: United Artists

SPARTACUS (U.S.A., 1959-1960; Bryna)
Executive Producer	Kirk Douglas
Producer	Edward Lewis
Director	Stanley Kubrick
Script	Dalton Trumbo, based on the book by Howard Fast
Photography	Russell Metty
Additional photography	Clifford Stine
Screen Process	Super Technirama-70
Color	Technicolor

Editors	Robert Lawrence
	Robert Schultz
	Fred Chulack
Production Designer	Alexander Golitzen
Art Director	Eric Orbom
Set decoration	Russell A. Gausman
	Julia Heron
Titles	Saul Bass
Technical Adviser	Vittorio Nino Novarese
Costumes	Peruzzi
	Valles
	Bill Thomas
Music	Alex North
Music Director	Joseph Gershenson
Sound	Waldon O. Watson
	Joe Lapis
	Murray Spivack
	Ronald Pierce

Kirk Douglas (Spartacus), Laurence Olivier (Marcus Crassus), Jean Simmons (Varinia), Charles Laughton (Gracchus), Peter Ustinov (Batiatus), John Gavin (Julius Caesar), Tony Curtis (Antoninus), Nina Foch (Helena), Herbert Lom (Tigranes), John Ireland (Crixus), John Dall (Glabrus), Charles McGraw (Marcellus), Joanna Barnes (Claudia), Harold J. Stone (David), Woody Strode (Draba), Peter Brocco (Ramon), Paul Lambert (Gannicus), Robert J. Wilke (Captain of Guard), Nicholas Dennis (Dionysius), John Hoyt (Roman Officer), Fred Worlock (Laelius), Dayton Lummis (Symmachus)
Original time: 196 minutes
Distributor: Universal Pictures

LOLITA (Great Britain, 1961; Seven Arts/Anya/Transworld)
Producer	James B. Harris
Director	Stanley Kubrick
Script	Vladimir Nabokov, based on his own novel
Photography	Oswald Morris
Editor	Anthony Harvey
Art Director	William Andrews
Set design	Andrew Low
Music	Nelson Riddle
Theme music	Bob Harris
Sound	H. L. Bird
	Len Shilton

James Mason (Humbert Humbert), Sue Lyon (Lolita Haze), Shelley Winters (Charlotte Haze), Peter Sellers (Clare Quilty), Diana Decker (Jean Farlow), Jerry Stovin (John Farlow), Suzanne Gibbs (Mona Farlow), Gary Cockrell (Dick), Marianne Stone (Vivian Darkbloom),

Cec Linder (physician), Lois Maxwell (Nurse Mary Lore), William Greene (Swine), C. Denier Warren (Potts), Isobel Lucas (Louise), Maxine Holden (receptionist), James Dyrenforth (Beale), Roberta Shore (Lorna), Eric Lane (Roy), Shirley Douglas (Mrs. Starch), Roland Brand (Bill), Colin Maitland (Charlie), Irvin Allen (hospital attendant), Marion Mathie (Miss Lebone), Craig Sams (Rex), John Harrison (Tom)
Time: 153 minutes
Distributor: Metro-Goldwyn-Mayer

DR. STRANGELOVE, OR HOW I LEARNED TO STOP WORRYING AND LOVE THE BOMB (Great Britain, 1963; Hawk Films)

Producer-Director	Stanley Kubrick
Associate Producer	Victor Lyndon
Script	Stanley Kubrick, Terry Southern, Peter George, based on the novel *Red Alert*, by Peter George
Photography	Gilbert Taylor
Editor	Anthony Harvey
Production Designer	Ken Adam
Art Director	Peter Murton
Special effects	Wally Veevers
Music	Laurie Johnson
Aviation Adviser	Captain John Crewdson
Sound	John Cox

Peter Sellers (Group Captain Lionel Mandrake, President Muffley, Dr. Strangelove), George C. Scott (General "Buck" Turgidson), Sterling Hayden (General Jack D. Ripper), Keenan Wynn (Colonel "Bat" Guano), Slim Pickens (Major T. J. "King" Kong), Peter Bull (Ambassador de Sadesky), Tracy Reed (Miss Scott), James Earl Jones (Lieutenant Lothar Zogg, bombardier), Jack Creley (Mr. Staines), Frank Berry (Lieutenant H. R. Dietrich, D.S.O.), Glenn Beck (Lieutenant W. D. Kivel, navigator), Shane Rimmer (Captain G. A. "Ace" Owens, copilot), Paul Tamarin (Lieutenant B. Goldberg, radio operator), Gordon Tanner (General Faceman), Robert O'Neil (Admiral Randolph), Roy Stephens (Frank), Laurence Herder, John McCarthy, Hal Galili (members of Burpelson Base Defense Corps)
Time: 94 minutes
Distributor: Columbia Pictures

2001: A SPACE ODYSSEY
(Great Britain, 1968; Metro-Goldwyn-Mayer)

Producer	Stanley Kubrick
Director	Stanley Kubrick
Script	Stanley Kubrick, Arthur C. Clarke, based on the

	latter's short story "The Sentinel"
Photography	Geoffrey Unsworth
Screen process	Super Panavision
	Presented in Cinerama
Color	Metrocolor
Additional photography	John Alcott
Special Photographic Effects Designer and Director	Stanley Kubrick
Editor	Ray Lovejoy
Production Designers	Tony Masters
	Harry Lange
	Ernie Archer
Art Director	John Hoesli
Special Photographic Effects Supervisors	Wally Veevers
	Douglas Trumbull
	Con Pederson
	Tom Howard
Music	Richard Strauss
	Johann Strauss
	Aram Khachaturian
	György Ligeti
Costumes	Hardy Amies
Sound	Winston Ryder

Keir Dullea (David Bowman), Garry Lockwood (Frank Poole), William Sylvester (Dr. Heywood Floyd), Daniel Richter (moonwatcher), Douglas Rain (voice of HAL 9000), Leonard Rossiter (Smyslov), Margaret Tyzack (Elena), Robert Beatty (Halvorsen), Sean Sullivan (Michaels), Frank Miller (Mission Control), Penny Brahms (stewardess), Alan Gifford (Poole's father), Ed Bishop, Glenn Beck, Edwina Carroll, Mike Lovell, Peter Delman, Dany Grover, Brian Hawley
Time: 141 minutes
Distributor: Metro-Goldwyn-Mayer

A CLOCKWORK ORANGE (Great Britain, 1971; Warner Brothers)
Producer	Stanley Kubrick
Director	Stanley Kubrick
Script	Stanley Kubrick, based on the novel by Anthony Burgess
Editor	Bill Butler
Music	Ludwig von Beethoven
	Henry Purcell
	Gioacchino Rossini
	Walter Carlos

Malcolm McDowell (Alex), Patrick McGee (Mr. Alexander), Adrienne
Corri (Mrs. Alexander), Aubrey Morris (Deltoid), James Marcus
(Georgie), Warren Clarke (Dim), Michael Tarn (Pete), Sheila Raynor
(Mum), Philip Stone (Dad), Miriam Karlin (Cat Lady), Godfrey Quig-
ley (Chaplain)
Time: 135 minutes
Distributor: Warner Brothers